I SOLVE MYSTERIES

THE ART AND SCIENCE OF BUSINESS PROCESS OPTIMIZATION AND TRANSFORMATION

PRAISE FOR
I SOLVE
MYSTERIES

"The objectives of almost every C-Suite executive is to increase sales and improve margins. This book is a must-read for any young leader or executive who have risen through the organization in sales, marketing, supply chain, operations, accounting or finance. *I Solve Mysteries* is a guidebook for self-analysis to improve operational efficiencies that will positively impact the bottom line."

George Kelley
Business Consultant and Former CEO of Pergo Flooring and SwissKrono USA

"It is gratifying to hear, as one of Dave's former professors, that what he took away from my class those many years ago has served him well throughout his career. *I Solve Mysteries* will help provide the next generation of professionals a wealth of experiences that should benefit them throughout their careers solving mysteries."

Michael Meeropol
Professor Emeritus, Western New England University

"In his new book, *I Solve Mysteries*; Dave Dragon leverages his extensive experience in business process optimization and transformation to provide primary but profound tools to early and mid-career leaders who are forced to drive and guide organizational change. Dave orchestrates a powerful combination of key elements, foundation, leadership, and structure with the appropriate emphasis on culture to achieve the desired results regardless of the size of your enterprise. This is a 'how-to' book that should be the centerpiece of your business weapons arsenal for your especially challenging turn-around projects."

Ray Leathers
Co-author of *Shut Up, Get Lean: How to Stop Simply Talking About Lean Manufacturing and Actually Start Building Your Culture of Continuous Improvement*

"Reading Dave Dragon's book is like sitting down with a wise sage over a cup of coffee and getting the 411 on how things work. Dave lays out the essentials of business process optimization, including what it is, why it's important, and how to drive it. He shares his personal journey and thought process about why businesses struggle with their current operating model and how to steer organizations toward better results. If you are just starting your career, taking on a role where business processes need work, or just seeking to understand how your unique skills do actually fit in a corporate environment, I recommend you take some time with Dave's book."

Chris Geissler
Technology, Innovation, and Business Strategy Consultant, MBA Professor and Startup Advisor

"*I Solve Mysteries* cuts through the mystique of business transformation! Dave Dragon does an excellent job of identifying both potential roadblocks and key success factors in an easily digestible format with an engaging writing style. The core concepts in this book are applicable to businesses of all sizes, and the book contains sound advice on how to maximize the odds of a successful project. I highly recommend *I Solve Mysteries* for any business leader considering a change initiative."

Greg Williams
MBA, GE Veteran, Experienced Business Consultant, and Former CEO

I SOLVE MYSTERIES

THE ART AND SCIENCE OF BUSINESS PROCESS OPTIMIZATION AND TRANSFORMATION

DAVE DRAGON

SILVER TREE
PUBLISHING

DEDICATION

To our Lord and Savior for blessing me with the intellect and an
inquisitive mind to solve complex mysteries.

To my wife and daughter, who loved and supported me through all
the nights I have spent on the road and away from home.

To my mother, for raising me with unconditional love.

"Everything we see hides another thing; we always want to see what is hidden by what we see."

René François Ghislain Magritte,
Belgian Surrealist, contemporary and
friend of Salvador Dalí

TABLE OF CONTENTS

CHAPTER 1

INTRODUCTION

I have been involved with some form of business process optimization and transformation since I held my position as a cost accountant in a manufacturing plant.

Fast forward in my career, and I have worked with a number of Fortune 100/500 clients and smaller organizations on business process optimization and transformation projects.

From my earliest beginnings in business process optimization and transformation to how I handle projects today, I have found that the #1 prerequisite for being successful at business process optimization and transformation is having an "inquisitive mind."

> **The #1 prerequisite for being successful at business process optimization and transformation is having an "inquisitive mind."**

What does it mean to have an inquisitive mind?

It means you have a personality given to identifying the unknown through inquiry, research, or asking questions.

You are eager for knowledge; you are intellectually curious.

You are a keen listener.

You can be inappropriately curious.

You are prying.

You make people uncomfortable with your questions.

You can get under people's skins with your curiosity.

You can be irritating.

Yep, that is me for sure.

If you don't have an inquisitive mind, you can stop right here because you will not have what it takes for business process optimization and transformation.

If you don't have an inquisitive mind, you can stop right here because you will not have what it takes for business process optimization and transformation.

When people ask me what I do for my profession, I tell them I specialize in business process optimization and transformation projects. In layman's terms: I help companies fix broken business processes in a variety of industries and business processes.

People who work in business can generally relate to a broken business process or business processes in their work environment.

It never ceases to amaze me how many people I talk with who are frustrated with their organizations for not fixing their broken business processes. Of course, some companies keep pace with changes in their business and update their business processes.

But many don't.

I then go onto explain just how I do what I do:

I am an **Archaeologist**, studying process activities through the analysis of artifacts. I research topics through data analysis to learn more about the past and present.

I am an **Anthropologist**, studying various aspects of organizational behavior within past and present. I research topics that include the discovery of norms that explore the social and cultural DNA of the organization.

I am a **Detective**, investigating the information I obtain through my work as an Anthropologist and Archaeologist by talking to witnesses, collecting more physical evidence, or searching records. I am examining and evaluating clues to uncover the true root cause of the business process problem. In other words: "I Solve Mysteries!"

I am a **Strategist**, responsible for the formulation and implementation of a business process optimization and transformation strategy. The strategy generally involves setting goals, determining actions to achieve the goals, and mobilizing resources to execute the actions.

I am a **Psychologist**, a mental health professional who evaluates and studies behavior and mental processes. I practice psychology, which is the science of behavior and the mind, including conscious and subconscious thought. My aim is to understand individuals and groups by establishing general principles and researching specific behavioral examples.

I am a **Psychiatrist**, specializing in the diagnosis, prevention, study and treatment of mental disorders. "Psychiatrists must evaluate patients to determine whether their symptoms are the result of a physical illness, a combination of physical and mental ailments, or strictly psychiatric."[1]

I am a **Conductor**, a Maestro, the person responsible for directing a performance. I perform the art of directing simultaneous performances of several players. As a Conductor, I interpret the score, set the tempo and manage the ensemble members.

There you have it, my 60-second elevator pitch on what I do and how I do it.

Methodologies

Do you have what it takes to excel at business process optimization and transformation?

You will find out as we go into greater detail in the upcoming chapters.

Optimization: An act, process, or methodology of making something (such as a design, system, or decision) as fully perfect, functional, or effective as possible.

Transformation: A change of variables in which a function of new variables is substituted for original variables, which results in a change of composition.

Art: Something that is created with imagination and skill, and that is beautiful, or that expresses important ideas or feelings.

Science: A systematic enterprise that builds and organizes knowledge in the form of testable explanations and predictions about the universe.[2]

I was working on business process optimization and transformation before consultants came up with names for how to define our work.

Activity-based management, Lean, Six Sigma, S&OP/Integrated Business Planning and Total Quality Management are all commonly used descriptions to define a methodology.

Were we doing activity-based management, Lean, Six Sigma, S&OP/Integrated Business Planning, and Total Quality Management before the consultants came up with what I call the "wrappers?" Of course we were.

Maybe not in the exact format that is defined by the current methodology, but in principle, we were following processes to correct problems, drive improvements and generate better profits.

1. Were we evaluating how many people and processes it took to perform certain jobs?
2. Were we looking at ways to make processes more efficient and take out waste?
3. Were we defining, measuring, analyzing, improving and controlling business processes?
4. Were we demand-planning and supply-planning while looking at financial impacts?
5. Were we working on a variety of ways to improve quality?

Yes, we were!

Did we have contexts, methodologies or wrappers to define our work? No, we were trying to make our companies operate more effectively and efficiently.

Do I have a problem with the methodology wrapper? Not at all.

If it can help structure a methodology into a more defined approach and assist people with being better organized, equipped, and more informed on how to present and learn the topics, all the better. Hey, I'm a Six Sigma Black Belt. I like that moniker, and I like the potential of what it can do to help the aim of projects!

Over time, better, and more advanced tools have been incorporated into methodologies. This has all been done to make our efforts in business process optimization and transformation more robust, scientific and value-driven.

Business process optimization and transformation is the accumulation of a lot of "moving parts" that include history, current state and future state elements.

Business process optimization and transformation is the accumulation of a lot of "moving parts" that include history, current state and future state elements.

Eight Key Elements

I have defined the moving parts by eight key elements that are the essentials for business process optimization and transformation projects.

1. The Foundation
2. Organization
3. Business Processes
4. Information Technology
5. Data, Master and Operational

6. Performance Management

7. Policies

8. Organizational Change Management

Think of the process in this way:

1. All of the "moving parts" — whether history, current state, or future state — must be integrated into a storyline that teams need to understand.

2. All this knowledge will be used as the basis for formulating how we are going from current state to future state.

3. Ask yourself: What are our strategies to effectively and efficiently move from our current state to our future state?

4. Determine, from current to future, how we are going to get to the future.

5. Now ask yourself: What does the future look like?

6. Honestly answer: Will I/we like the future or fear it?

7. Assess: How hard will it be to get to the future?

These are all good questions to ask ourselves because the Psychologist getting the organization from the current state to the future state can be our biggest challenge.

Getting the organization to move forward from the current state to the future state takes a concerted effort to mobilize the troops.

To understand how we are going to move forward, we will look at history as defined by our work as the Anthropologist, Archaeologist and Detective.

The knowledge we gain through this analysis will be used to develop our strategy (or strategies) as a Strategist and our approach as the Psychologist as it relates to organizational change management.

In a few rare cases, we must work as a Psychiatrist, because sometimes we run into crazy people!

Make no mistake about it; a robust organizational change management program is required to get from the current state to the future state! In keeping with that spirit; this is how I have structured the chapters of this book:

Book Structure

1. **The Foundation**: We will cover the definition and relevance of the executive sponsorship, steering committee, project manager, project teams, charters, project plan and RACI (Responsible, Accountable, Consulted, Informed) Matrix.

2. **Organization**: We will cover the organizational structure, executive sponsor and steering committee, project manager and project team, and the organizational culture as well as introduce concepts in change management.

3. **Business Processes**: We will cover the process methodologies I have used on business process optimization and transformation projects. I have included four narratives about my optimization and transformation experiences.

4. **Information Technology and Master Data**: We will cover subjects around information technology and the importance of data governance.

5. **Performance Management and Operational Data**: We will cover my perspectives on performance management and the importance of data quality.

6. **Policies**: We will cover what governs decisions.

7. **Organizational Change Management**: We will cover the elements of a change management program.

8. **Artificial Intelligence, Machine Learning, Robotic Process Automation, Predictive and Prescriptive Analytics**: We will cover the new frontier in business process optimization and transformation.

Along the way, we will be solving mysteries! Some simple, some complex.

Why I Do What I Do, Why I Love What I Do

I have been involved with business process optimization and transformation my entire career.

When I first started this type of work, it was positively for self-promotion, as I was establishing my business credentials and progression in my career. I was "the guy" who was sent to fix a variety of problems and who built a reputation of being able to fix just about anything. That association brought with it some personal challenges as I was not always welcome.

In many cases, the people I worked with didn't appreciate having someone identify what was wrong and explain to them what they needed to do to remedy the situation.

As I mentioned, I was and am still a pain when it comes to asking probing questions and getting under people's skin.

In my defense, I come by the habit naturally and with no ill will. My auditing training as an accountant taught me to ask so many questions! *Damn, auditors!*

My focus has now changed to "What can I do for others?" It's not so much about me anymore; it's about how I can have a positive impact on people's jobs, and their job satisfaction and lives.

> **It's not so much about me anymore; it's about how I can have a positive impact on people's jobs, and their job satisfaction and lives.**

When I start a project, I see so much frustration, anger and disappointment because people cannot see a way out of their current circumstances. Besides, frustration, anger and disappointment, there is a significant amount of *fear*. Fear about the sustainability of their current circumstances and fear about what the future will hold.

I can't guarantee there will be no negative impact on people's job statuses. But what I find in most cases, is a positive impact on job status and satisfaction. That is what motivates me now, helping others. And that is the intention of this book, to help you in your career, too!

I work hard to take away my clients' frustration, anger, disappointment and fear by giving them a positive path forward. By giving them a vision and place in the future where they will feel good about their jobs. Where the future is a positive environment, and the current state is long forgotten.

I want to make positive impacts on people's careers and lives through the work I do.

It is always so gratifying when people see the first glimmer of hope and opportunity for the future. The future is not such a scary place. It's actually a place of encouragement and opportunity, where you can see the energy both returning to individuals and flowing toward the future.

Why I Wrote *I Solve Mysteries*

Please let me start out by saying that I have not authored a book before. Authoring a book has been a totally new experience. An enjoyable and enlightening experience. An enjoyable and enlightening experience with the awesome help and guidance from the team at Silver Tree Publishing.

Secondly, I would like to thank all my colleagues and clients that have been so integral to my career and the optimization and transformation projects. I have learned and grown through working with all of you.

Where do I begin about why I authored *I Solve Mysteries*?

Let's start with some history.

Over the past many years, I have worked on a number of optimization and transformation projects with a number of early-career and mid-career professionals, both on the consulting side and client side. Many of these professionals had never been exposed to a significant optimization or transformation project.

What dawned on me last year was that there were no education materials that explained the ins and outs of optimization and transformation projects to these professionals.

Many times, they are assigned to an optimization and transformation project and expected to learn as they go.

It also dawned on me that I was seeing the same lack of education with steering committees that were managing these projects. Leaders on steering committees have demanding jobs guiding their organizations and departments. Being assigned to a steering committee on a large optimization or transformation project can be a new experience for them.

Optimization and transformation projects are usually cross-functional in nature. Getting R&D, marketing, sales, supply chain, operations, accounting and IT on the same page is paramount.

Because, depending on the project, one or more or many of these departments will all be going through the journey together. And we all know how well cross-functional communication works in most companies.

The genesis of *I Solve Mysteries* is that through better education, knowledge and preparation, optimization and transformation projects would go much smoother and avoid the common pitfalls that these projects experience.

As a process guy, my gut was telling me there was a better way to prepare early-career and mid-career professionals and steering committees about the dynamics of these projects in a more structured way.

I Solve Mysteries follows a structure for projects that has evolved over many years and many projects. It has evolved and matured as I have worked with different consulting and technology organizations and clients on a variety of optimization and transformation projects in a variety of industries.

As I was contemplating writing the book last year, I started to "test drive" some of the concepts I thought would be educational and entertaining to readers. I received great feedback and support from the professionals I was working with on the projects.

Looking to gather additional input, I reached out to my professional and personal network, continuing to test my concepts.

The response was very positive with everyone giving me a green light and thumbs up for the book.

As I was writing the book, I asked myself: *"What do you actually do on optimization and transformation projects?"*

Well it dawned on me that I am constantly "Solving Mysteries." I am constantly solving organization, culture, business process, information technology, data, performance management and policy mysteries all through the project.

Every 5-10 years, there is a quantum leap in technology when the hardware, software, data and knowledge catch up with the vision. That is where we are today with artificial intelligence (AI), machine learning (ML), robotic process automation (RPA) and prescriptive analytics (PA).

If you have been in technology long enough, you know that artificial intelligence, machine learning, robotic process automation and prescriptive analytics are evolutionary not revolutionary.

Many of the same challenges we have faced in the past will need to be addressed today and in the near future as AI, ML, RPA and PA become more main stream and adoption begins to accelerate.

And in many cases the challenges will be magnified.

Whether you are looking at a traditional optimization or transformation project or one based on artificial intelligence, machine learning, robotic process automation and prescriptive analytics, you still need a strategy and plan to prepare and mobilize the organization for success.

Optimization or transformation is more than an ambitious aim — it requires a plan and diligent commitment.

And so we have *I Solve Mysteries: The Art and Science of Business Process Optimization and Transformation*. Because solving mysteries is as much art as it is science.

CHAPTER 2

THE FOUNDATION

Some foundation elements need to be in place before you start an optimization or transformation project. That's why I'm starting this chapter talking about the executive sponsor because the person in this seat has such critical importance to the success or failure of the project.

What You Need to Build a Successful Foundation

Every project needs an executive sponsor.

Let's now turn our attention to the steering committee because it holds another critical role and is in charge of additional critical responsibilities to the project.

The organizational leaders who are on or not on the steering committee can provide useful insights into the culture of the organization.

The executive sponsor and steering committee provide the governance on the project.

When important guidance and decisions are required to keep the project on track, the executive sponsor and steering committee must execute their fiduciary responsibilities for the project.

The project manager and project team are responsible for the daily execution of the project.

Selecting the correct project manager and populating the project team sets a clear tone for the organization as to the importance of the optimization or transformation of the project.

> **Selecting the correct project manager and populating the project team sets a clear tone for the organization as to the importance of the optimization or transformation of the project.**

Next, the administrative part of the project, the project charter is a foundation document. The charter explains the importance of the project and why it's being undertaken. It provides the governance criteria that will be used by the executive sponsor and steering committee in their fiduciary responsibilities.

The project plan details the activities of the various project work-streams and is aligned with the resources and timeline to complete the project. Projects can be subject to what is called "scope creep," which I explain in greater detail in a later portion of the book. What's helpful to remember is that the project plan provides the executive sponsor, steering committee and project manager, an important governance system to manage the progress of the project, and an understanding of potential conflicts and impact if scope creep is identified.

Executive Sponsor

If anything is the most important element to a business process optimization and transformation project, it is executive sponsorship.

When I say, "executive sponsorship," I am talking about the board, chairman, president, chief executive officer (CEO), or chief operating officer (COO).

> When I say, "executive sponsorship," I am talking about the board, chairman, president, chief executive officer (CEO), or chief operating officer (COO).

The scope and size of the business process optimization and transformation project will help guide the organization toward knowing which level likely has the best candidates to be your executive sponsor.

It is a proven fact, many times over, that without engaged executive sponsorship, large-scale optimization and transformation projects fail. This is why the organization needs to take care in choosing who will be its executive sponsor.

Even with an executive sponsor, large-scale optimization and transformation projects will fail when the executive sponsor is absent, or negligent in their duties.

The best business optimization and transformation projects I have delivered have been as a result of the executive sponsor being fully engaged yet not bogged down in the details. Meaning, they are both running on all cylinders for the project and knowledgeable about the status of the project. They also have a keen understanding of key issues that have been identified, and they have been involved with the key decisions themselves.

I have been on projects where the executive sponsor has not been fully engaged, or knowledgeable about the status of the project; they did not have a keen understanding of key issues and were not involved with the key decisions. These projects have not been successful or as successful as they could have been.

Why is this so important? The executive sponsor sets the stage for change. The executive sponsor sets the tone for going from the current state to the future state. Now, before we go further, let me state, the organizational change management chapter is near the end of the book. However, you will see me blend change management into every nook and cranny throughout these pages. A lot of organizations and leaders don't get the organizational change management workstream. They don't want to understand organizational change management, or they might even think organizational change management is a waste of time. Nothing could be further from the truth! If the executive sponsor does not buy into the organizational change management workstream, you and the project are destined for a mediocre result or failure. You might as well pack up your bags. Conversely, you could keep going in a frustrated state and in many cases be blamed for the mediocre result or failure of the project. But, I digress, and promise you that we will cover these scenarios in later chapters of this book.

Executive sponsors need to lead and make decisions. Because inevitably, the project will reach a point where you have uncovered some unexpected issues (mysteries) that are the true root cause of the problem the team is addressing. Many of these issues will be either upstream or downstream from the process you are trying to transform. Also, some of the issues may be so fundamentally severe that only the executive sponsor will have the authority to approve the change in direction!

On one transformation project I was leading, the executive sponsor, the CEO, was absent. He was just not checked into what was going on. We provided the project leader counsel that the CEO needed to be more involved. He said he would take care of it but never did. Other members of the organization's leadership team were on the steering committee and were going to be impacted by the new program we were designing and implementing. A lot was going on at the company while we were designing and implementing the new program. Understandably, the CEO had a lot on his plate at the time, so he delegated decisions to the steering committee and members of his leadership team.

You can imagine how that went.

The leadership team checked out of the project. They canceled a few steering committee meetings due to lack of attendance. Because the program had a huge cross-functional transformational impact on the organization, some major decisions had to be made, but because of turf wars and protectionism, the correct decisions were not made. The project leader struggled to get the steering committee, who were members of the executive leadership team, participating in the monthly meetings — first, when we were in the beta mode and then when we went live.

Would I consider this project a failure? No, because the program we implemented brought a lot of significant value to the business.

Was it optimized for success? Was it truly transformational? No, not really.

Sure, we got the client moving in the right direction, but it was not an optimal situation that would have brought maximum benefit to the organization.

The key takeaway is that you need an executive sponsor, or more accurately, an *engaged* executive sponsor. Consider the risks and possible pitfalls. Remember, the executive sponsor sets the tone for change.

Remember, the executive sponsor sets the tone for change.

Steering Committee

The project steering committee is the governing body made up of key executive stakeholders that steer/guide and empower key project leaders to execute the project to a successful conclusion.

One of the executives on the steering committee should be assigned the position of the head of the steering committee. This position comes with management responsibilities to oversee the activities of the steering committee. The head of the steering committee is assigned this responsibility by the executive sponsor.

"Steering" is the key word. Steering is not managing. The managing is done by the project manager and project team. This is an important distinction to remember.

The steering committee steers/guides against the project charter that details the vision or underlying purpose of the project. When executing the project to the charter, they monitor and maintain oversight against deliverables and timelines of the project plan.

The role of the steering committee is to mediate conflicts, make deci-sions, advise, provide strategic oversight and serve as the primary advocate for the project manager and project team.

"Steering" is the key word. Steering is not managing. The managing is done by the project manager and project team. This is an important distinction to remember.

One of the most import roles of the steering committee is to manage against scope creep. "Scope creep," in project management, refers to changes, and continuous or uncontrolled growth in a project's scope, at any point after the project begins. This can occur when the scope of a project is not properly defined, documented, or controlled."[3]

That's why you need a strong project charter. Guardrails should be put into place to monitor against scope creep. Guardrails are a system designed to keep the project from straying into dangerous or off-limits areas (i.e., scope creep). Projects do need some "wiggle room," and that's where the guardrails are helpful, too. They func-tion as the threshold for allowable modifications. They provide the support and protective limitation or a boundary against scope creep.

Sometimes scope creep is inevitable, not because the project was not clearly defined, but because during the project "unexpected" infor-mation/knowledge (mysteries) is uncovered which clearly requires addressing in the project. At this stage, the steering committee must revisit the project charter to determine if the new informa-tion requires a revision to the charter. This may be one of the most important decisions that the steering committee will have to make, and the decision must not be taken lightly.

Which is like stating the obvious.

Changes to the project charter have huge ramifications concerning people, timeline and costs of the project. The steering committee must approve any significant changes to the project charter and then submit the "change request" to the executive sponsor who must approve or disapprove the updated project charter. In the project charter, the steering committee's "level of authority" must be clearly defined.

So, what decisions can the steering committee make relative to the project scope? And what decisions can't they make? If you want the answers to these questions, then project guardrails must be defined, and authority levels given.

Executives assigned to the steering committee usually "nominate" members of the project team. We have seen where companies have staffed their project teams with less sophisticated employees from the organization.

This is not a good idea, as there is well-documented history of many project failures due to team members that could not "step up" to manage the requirements of the project. Executives don't want to pull their "A-Players" out of their "functional areas" for fear that the performance of these functional areas will deteriorate without the A-Player in place. That said, if the project is important enough, then it should be made up of some A-Players.

Optimization and transformation projects can be an excellent learning opportunity when A-Players mentor other project team members who lack the sophistication to deliver projects on their own.

Engagement by members of the steering committee is paramount. Being engaged is a promise, that for a period of time, the steering committee executive is to be betrothed to the project. Membership

on the steering committee requires full executive engagement.
A successfully implemented project requires executive engagement.

However, getting executives engaged in the steering committee can
at times be like herding cats. Their roles and responsibilities must be
clearly defined, and their involvement articulated, monitored and
measured to be successful. If they fall short of their responsibilities,
it is up to the head of the steering committee to provide counsel. If
engagement does not improve, the head of the steering committee
must bring this to the attention of the executive sponsor.

This is a good time to note that the project team, in most cases, is
made up of middle management and takes its direction from its executives. If they see an executive who shows a lack of engagement, is
inactive or invisible or who promotes competing agendas, their level
of support will likely erode over time.

This kind of behavior by a member of the steering committee has
derailed a number of optimization and transformation projects.

- Steering committee executives need to share the same core
  values around the project.
- Steering committee executives should not have to be tightly
  managed. They should be active and visible.
- Steering committee executives need to do what they say they will
  do. There is no place for competing agendas.
- Steering committee executives need to understand that their
  responsibility is leadership.
- Steering committee executives need to understand that the
  project will most likely require cross-functional collaboration.
  The weakest link on the project will cause collateral damage.
- Steering committee executives need to be passionate concerning
  the optimization or transformation project.

The Project Manager and Project Team

Successful projects are the result of careful planning, top talent and the collaboration of a project's team members.

One of the most important decisions that the steering committee will make is the selection of the project manager. The project manager orchestrates all aspects of the project. They must be a person who is respected in the organization. Strong organizational, planning and execution skills are paramount.

It has been my experience that it has been beneficial for project managers to have some functional understanding of the optimization and transformation area. Being well-versed in the area, understanding of the challenges being faced in optimization and transformation, is even better. However, they must also be able to use an "independent and objective lens" to look through when managing the project.

The project manager holds the primary management role in the project and is responsible for its successful completion. Their responsibility is to ensure the project adheres to the project plan timeline and deliverables, and that they manage the expenses to deliver the project within the established budget while achieving the objectives of the project charter.

Project managers ensure that the project is given sufficient resources while managing relationships with the project team and the steering committee.

Project manager duties:

- Develop and maintain a project plan

- Manage project deliverables
- Recruit the project team
- Lead and manage the project team
- Identify and manage risks
- Provide monthly updates to the steering committee

A well-designed project team is made up of a cross-functional group of subject matter experts (SMEs) that have a strength within their particular functional areas such as sales, customer service, supply chain, operations, transportation, finance or information technology. They are sought out by others for their specialized knowledge. SMEs are usually the A-Players of a functional area. They engender a deep level of knowledge and respect from their peers.

As I mentioned before, you want as many A-Players on the project team. Project teams on optimization and transformation projects also make great testing grounds for up-and-coming, early-career leaders. I greatly enjoy the passion, enthusiasm, energy and fresh thoughts the early-career leaders bring to projects. They come with different perspectives.

As I explained, my focus now is, "What can I do for others?" Being able to work with and mentor these early-career and mid-career leaders fulfills my mission. I am writing this book in large part for them.

I want to transfer the knowledge and experiences I have accumulated over many years through the multiple optimization and transformation project experiences I am sharing in this book.

I aim to educate and train others in the art and science of business process optimization and transformation. This is now my passion.

Finally, an important consideration when designing a project team is whether you will use only internal resources or whether you need to bring in outside consultants.

In many cases, you will have to bring in consultants as your organization may not have the knowledge or skill sets to deliver the project. Consultants can play a critical role in the project team. They bring with them considerable knowledge and experience spanning multiple clients and industries who have participated in similar optimization and transformation projects. They can also be very valuable as "independent contributors" who are not caught up in internal politics and so can provide objective observation and direction.

Forming, Storming, Norming, Performing

Leading and managing the project team is obviously one of the key responsibilities of the project manager. Let me also say, a group development model is critical to managing the project team responsibilities.

> A group development model is critical to managing the project team responsibilities.

Maybe you have heard of the group development model called: Forming, Storming, Norming, Performing? It was first proposed by Bruce Tuckman.[4] "Tuckman said that these phases are all necessary and inevitable for the team to grow, face up to challenges, tackle problems, find solutions, plan work and deliver results."[5]

The project manager must be trained to understand this model to lead and manage the team effectively.

Forming

During this phase, the project team meets and learns about the project goals, project timeline, project deliverables and project team.

Project team members tend to behave quite independently when in the Forming stage. They may be motivated but are still relatively uninformed about the project goals, project timeline and project deliverables.

Team members are usually on their best behavior but are also very focused on themselves.

Storming

Storming is the second stage of team development when the group starts to sort itself out and gain each other's trust.

This stage often starts when members voice their opinions about the project. Conflict may arise between team members. Individual working styles are discovered. During this stage, a positive and polite atmosphere is evident. People are pleasant to each other, and they may have different feelings of excitement and eagerness. Others may have feelings of suspicion, fear and anxiety. Disagreements and personality clashes must begin to be resolved before the team can progress out of this stage.

Project team leaders and followers will begin to develop in the Storming phase.

Norming

Disagreements and personality clashes are resolved in Norming.

Project team members understand their responsibilities and develop the common ground to work together for the success of the project. They accept others as they are and make an effort to move on.

Performing

Project team members are focused on achieving project goals and often reach an unexpectedly high level of success.

By this time, members are motivated, knowledgeable and competent. Occasional dissent is expected and allowed as long as it is managed by the project manager to the project team's satisfaction.

Steering Committees will also go through the same team development of: Forming, Storming, Norming, Performing. Members of the Steering Committee may never have participated in an optimization or transformation project. They will experience the same cross-functional team dynamics as the project team.

As Steering Committees come together for the project, they have to find the same team footing as the project team. It is very important for Steering Committees to know that they are in the same developmental mode as the project team.

Another important role of the Steering Committee, as part of their duties, is to evaluate the development of the project team. If the project team is stuck in the Storming stage, they will never get to the Norming and Performing stage and the project will suffer.

Project Charter

As previously defined, the project charter is a statement of scope, objectives and people that are participating in a project. It is prepared by the steering committee and project manager and defines the roles and responsibilities of all participants as it outlines the objectives, progress and goals of the project. The project charter guides in project decision-making.

Once approved by the executive sponsor, the project charter authorizes the project to move forward.

Project Name and Description

The project name should provide a clear description of the project. Some organizations like to give the project a name like "Kilimanjaro." I prefer to keep the names simple and straightforward. But if your organization is inclined to be symbolic, give it a go.

The description of the project is brief and better described as a 60-second elevator pitch. A great question to strive to answer is how do I best describe the project in 60 seconds?

Business Case

The business case is a more descriptive commentary that explains:

- Why the project is being undertaken.
- What issues and pain points need to be remedied?
- What the objectives are.
- What the scope or boundaries are.
- How the project aligns with the strategic initiative(s) of the organization.
- What the internal and external resource requirements are.
- What the financial and non-financial impacts are.

Budget

Guidelines on budget commitments and thresholds need to be defined.

Goals/Deliverables

A preliminary set of goals and deliverables must be identified.

Key performance indicators (KPIs) are used to monitor project progress.

Team Roles and Responsibilities

Internal

- Executive sponsor
- Steering committee leader and members
- Project manager
- Internal SMEs by functional area
- Business analyst by functional area
- Administrative team

External – Consultant

- Executive sponsor
- Project manager
- SMEs by functional area
- Business analyst by functional area
- Administrative team

Risks and Constraints

The project charter should state known risks (as well as maintain a risk register) and constraints.

Guardrails

There should be an explanation of what guardrails have been established to guide the steering committee and project team relative to managing project scope and potential scope creep.

Timeline and Milestones

This is a high-level document outlining the timeline with the major milestones included and start and end dates provided.

Project Plan

The project plan is a steering-committee-approved document that guides the project manager and project team in the execution and management of the project. The project plan details the activities of the various project workstreams aligned with the resources and timeline to complete the project.

The project plan can be considered the "project roadmap."

The project plan answers these questions:

- What is the work required to complete the project?
- What are the project deliverables?
- Who is responsible for completing the work?
- When will the work be completed?

I will admit that I am not a project manager, although I have had to function in that capacity on certain projects.

As I mentioned, I prefer project managers who have an understanding of the business and the impact the project will have on the business. A functional project manager may need assistance with the administrative side of project management. *That is me; I need administrative help!* In this situation, you can educate and train junior staff on the principles and methodology of project management. This is quite an opportunity and is also a valuable learning experience for the junior staff. Those holding the business analyst or administrative roles in the project can take on the responsibilities to maintain and manage the project plan for the project manager.

> **A functional project manager may need assistance with the administrative side of project management. *That is me; I need administrative help!***

If the goal of the organization is to develop certified project managers, the Project Management Institute (PMI) provides certification as a Project Management Professional (PMP).

The Project Management Body of Knowledge (PMBOK) is a set of standard terminology and guidelines for project management published by the Project Management Institute (PMI).[6]

A number of software tools are useful in developing your project plan as well. They include Microsoft Project, JIRA, Smartsheet, Zoho, Planview and Podio, to name a few.

I would say the dominant PM tool, not listed above, that I have seen used is Excel.

When encouraging the development of your team, take a moment to consider all your options and which ones would be best for your team.

RACI (Responsible, Accountable, Consulted, Informed) Matrix

Once you have the steering committee and project team established, developing a RACI Matrix[7] is imperative. RACI is a valuable exercise and tool used to manage the project. A RACI Matrix or chart is a tool that identifies roles and responsibilities against objectives within a project. As noted previously, RACI stands for: Responsible, Accountable, Consulted and Informed.

The RACI maps objectives and deliverables against the roles, decision-making and responsibilities of your project.

Many people get confused between the "R," Responsible, and the "A," Accountable. The highest level of authority and ownership is the "A," Accountable. But because the "A" comes after the "R," many think the "R" represents the ownership. But that is not the case. In RACI, because the "A" is Accountable, it has the authority and ownership. Another way of looking at the structure is that there can only be one "A," but the "R" can occur multiple times.

"R" is Responsible for Doing the Work

The person or persons assigned the "R" is responsible for executing the objective or deliverable. Depending on the objective, one or more people can occupy an "R" role. They are responsible for getting the work done and, in some cases, making a decision. It doesn't matter how many people are in an "R" role either. Everyone must uphold their responsibilities.

As an example, if the objective is inventory optimization, an "R" may be assigned to planning, purchasing, operations and finance professionals.

"A" is Accountable and the Owner of the Objective

This person or role is responsible for the overall completion of the objective or deliverable. They won't get the work done but are the *owner* for making sure it is completed. The "A" role is assigned to one person to avoid confusion over who actually owns the "O," the objective.

In the objective above — inventory optimization — the accountable person is the chief supply chain officer (CSCO).

To further clarify or confuse you, the objective is inventory optimization, but there may be a higher-level goal to increase earnings before interest, taxes, depreciation and amortization (EBITDA).[8] If this is the case, the CSCO has the "R" responsible role, and the COO has the "A" accountable role.

The way that we would combine the "R" or "A" roles is dependent on the objective or goal.

"C" is Consulted and Asked-for Guidance or Specialized Inputs

This person(s), will provide information useful for completing the objective or deliverable. Two-way communication between those responsible and those consulted is paramount.

In the example above, the chief technology officer (CTO), may be consulted for inputs on old and slow-moving raw materials. Or the chief sales officer (CSO), may be consulted for old and slow-moving finished goods.

"I" is Informed and Kept Aware

These people or groups will be kept up-to-date on the objective or deliverable. Communication could happen as the project progresses, or when the objective or deliverable is completed.

An "I" won't be asked for feedback or review, but they can be affected by the outcome of the task or deliverable.

In the above example, the chief marketing officer (CMO), would be informed of the progress of inventory optimization.

The Advantages of a RACI

1. Streamlining Communication

Having a RACI in place can be useful to refer back to throughout the life of a project.

Rather than involving every single person in every single decision, you can streamline the communication, involve the right people at the right time and speed up sign-offs and decision making.

2. One Clear Accountable

You know where the buck stops, with one owner, the "A." This is where a RACI is very useful. A clear distinction between the Responsible, Accountable, Consulted and Informed is prevalent.

A distinct separation concerning those involved in doing the work, those whose expertise is sought out and those who are updated on progress on the objective is enabled.

3. Setting Clear Expectations

You can create a lot of efficiencies using a RACI chart on your project. When you create a RACI at the beginning of a project, it can be useful to help set expectations for who is managing or responsible for specific work going forward.

People involved in the project should be able to clearly see where they need to be involved, and with what tasks. RACIs can also help eliminate confusion by identifying who is ultimately accountable for an objective or deliverable completion.

Note: It's particularly useful to set expectations with more senior stakeholders who are informed on the project. It will allow them to know what information they will receive as part of the project.

Summary

The foundation is what sets the tone for the project. Have you dotted every "i" and crossed every "t"? Getting the foundation put into place is critical to any project's success.

Whether you are optimizing or transforming business processes or building a 70-story condominium, the foundation is what brings stability to the project. It guides your ability to govern and make informed decisions.

Are we solving mysteries yet? You bet we are — *because solving mysteries begins with the foundation.*

Are we solving mysteries yet? You bet we are — *because solving mysteries begins with the foundation.*

Your perspective of the mysteries may be a bit different depending on whether you are an internal resource from the organization or an outside consultant.

But there are still mysteries to be solved:

- Why was this person selected to be the executive sponsor?
- Why are these the members of the steering committee?
- Why was this person selected to be the project manager?
- Why are these the members of the project team?
- Why has the project charter been written this way?
- Why has the executive sponsor and steering committee approved this project plan?

We are solving mysteries over the life of the project.

CHAPTER 3
ORGANIZATION

The organizational side of business process optimization and transformation is pretty complex, with a lot of subject areas and moving parts. You have to immerse yourself and the project team in understanding the complexities and nuances of the organization because the project team, your organization and you will find out information you thought you knew, but in actuality, did not.

> You have to immerse yourself and the project team in understanding the complexities and nuances of the organization because the project team, your organization and you will find out information you thought you knew, but in actuality, did not.

There are a lot of mysteries to solve in organizations!

Let's Begin with the Iterative Process

Understanding the organization and its dynamics is an iterative process. As the project progresses, new information is identified, and decisions must be made. You will see organizational dynamics unfold in front of you, and in many cases, what you learn will be very different than what you expected to learn.

You will see that iterative processes will be used time and again throughout the areas we'll discuss. The iterative process or iteration is the act of repeating a process, in our case, knowledge gathering, multiple times with the goal of determining whether the information you have gathered is consistent and factual. Each time you repeat the process, it is called an "iteration." The results of the last iteration are used as the starting point for the next iteration.

The iterative process is similar to a concept called "peeling back the layers of an onion." Each layer of the onion is an iteration. As you peel back each layer, ask yourself, "Is the information from the previous layer consistent?"

You will find some parts of the information will be *consistent*, but you will also discover information that *clarifies* information from the previous layer, as well as you will find information that *contradicts* what you have learned from a previous layer. That is the whole point of multiple iterations.

You want to progress to where the information is consistent and factual.

You want to progress to where the information is consistent and factual.

Later in the book, we will discuss a Six Sigma tool, and the 5 Whys[9], which is also a form of iteration that you can use instead of the onion concept.

It's important to remember that the iterative process gets to the root causes that affect the process(s) under optimization and transformation. You'll be using iterative processes to determine the root cause across all the elements of the optimization and transformation project.

Root Cause Analysis and Symptoms

Root cause analysis (RCA) is a method of problem-solving used for identifying the root causes of faults or problems.

A problem area is considered a root cause if its removal *really* solves the problem. When you remove the root cause, the corrective action will eliminate the problem from recurring.

Most times, the people you work with will give you symptoms of the issues(s). A symptom is a subjective piece of evidence of a problem or an issue. It is an indication that something is wrong.

For example, as I write this book, my right shoulder hurts. I am in pain. This is a symptom of an injury. I'll need to go to the doctor for a diagnosis of what is the root cause of my pain.

As the Archaeologist and Anthropologist, symptoms will provide you information about artifacts and cultural issues that we will use in root cause analysis. Our work as the Detective is to diagnose symptoms/ evidence to lead us to the root cause of the problem area.

Think of it as if we were solving a mystery! We are lucky to consider ourselves a Sherlock Holmes, Hercule Poirot and even a Clouseau of the business world!

Think of it as if we were solving a mystery! We are lucky to consider ourselves a Sherlock Holmes, Hercule Poirot and even a Clouseau of the business world!

I hope you can see that our work as the Archaeologist and Anthropologist provides us evidence or symptoms that we'll use when we put on our hat as the Detective solving the mystery.

A Real-Life Example

I worked on a very complex transformation project several years ago. The organization, business processes, technology, performance management, policy and controls and change management indicated a ton of symptoms. After all the work we undertook to diagnose the wide variety of symptoms, yet we kept coming back to the same root cause. It was complex and had a lot of variabilities. We found it was a huge undertaking to remedy that root cause!

We had to involve marketing, sales, finance and the C-suite to make the decisions needed to remedy the root cause.

Talk about change management!

But that's a story for another day; let's get back to talking about organization.

Now, we'll continue to explore the areas of organizational structure, organizational culture, organizational leadership, steering committee and organizational ownership.

Organizational Structure

It never ceases to amaze me that companies don't have up-to-date organizational charts.

I can't tell you how many times I will ask a client for a current organizational chart, only to have them say they will have to get back to me, or they will have to check with HR.

Yes, you will need an up-to-date organizational chart before you get started.

You may think you know your organization, and you very well might, but I will venture a bet you will find out there are parts you do not fully understand. Whether you are running the business process optimization and transformation project yourself or with consultants, you will want an up-to-date organizational chart.

The first things I try to understand from the organizational chart are:

- Who is the executive sponsor?
- Who from the leadership team is on the steering committee?
- Who is the steering committee leader?
- Who from the leadership team is not on the steering committee?
- Who is the project manager?
- Who is on the project team?

You may think you know the reporting lines, but in my experience, many project managers have stated with a puzzled look on their faces, "I did not know that person reported to..."

I think you get the point.

1.   Who is the Executive Sponsor?

As the Anthropologist, I am looking at culture.

I must know how high in the organization have we gone to place the executive sponsor?

Is this a board-level optimization and transformation project, or are we at the president/CEO or COO level? If we are at the board level, then this is a really big deal. The optimization and transformation project have the eyes and the ears of the board of directors. It does not mean we will interact with the board of directors, but it does mean they will provide a certain level of oversight. The president/CEO, in their capacity as the steering committee leader/chair will most likely be interacting with the board.

If the executive sponsor is at the president/CEO level, we have to know who is this person? Is the president/CEO a long-term employee? Were they brought in recently by the board to "right the ship?" What is the president/CEO's DNA — is he/she a functional expert in sales, finance, or operations, for example? This knowledge is important and will be needed as you move through the project when decisions have to be made. If the president/CEO is a long-term employee, they are embedded in the culture of the organization. They have been part of the team that has established the culture of the organization. They may have several long-term friends on the leadership team who are members of the steering committee.

If the president/CEO has been recently brought in to "right the ship," they may be working to change the culture. They may have brought in their friends to be on the leadership team, or they may be at odds with long-term employees on the leadership team.

If the executive sponsor is below CEO-level in the organization, say, they are a COO, chief supply chain officer or a chief financial officer, how effective will they be in managing up to the CEO-level and across with the C-suite colleagues?

2. Who from the Leadership Team is on the Steering Committee?

Most if not all, optimization and transformation projects will have a cross-functional impact on the organization. The makeup of the steering committee indicates whether the organization understands how cross-functional the optimization and transformation project really is. When you are first starting the project, you may not know all the areas the project will touch.

3. Who from the Leadership Team is not on the Steering Committee?

This relates to item #2 and indicates whether the organization understands how cross-functional the optimization and transformation project really is.

I was on a project where there was no supply chain leadership represented on the steering committee. When I was just starting the project, I did not know if this was going to be an issue. Early on in the current state analysis, we found that the symptoms were indicating effects on the supply chain.

Before I continue with this story, you should know, current state analysis or as-is analysis documents the current status of how the process or business operates.

When we started to engage with the supply chain leadership, they were standoffish, to say the least. Actually, they were *pissed* that they were not included in the project on the steering committee.

A number of symptoms pointed to the supply chain, but the supply chain leadership still never really engaged.

This is the type of political consequence you can face in the project. When you exclude certain functions from the steering committee, and the project ultimately intersects with them, you'll have a huge change management hurdle to overcome. Instead of being an active participant, specific representatives of specific departments can become a casual observer. When this is the case, you can expect that they might never really engage with the project. If there is a lack of engagement, and it is a pivotal functional area related to the future solution design, you have put yourself into a deep hole.

If there is a lack of engagement, and it is a pivotal functional area related to the future solution design, you have put yourself into a deep hole.

Trying to regain their trust, commitment and participation can be an uphill battle. This can have a significant effect on the project timeline if their input is critical to the overall success of the project.

Before building out the steering committee, some companies take the step to perform a stakeholder analysis to improve the process for selecting steering committee members. A stakeholder analysis is frequently used during the preparation phase of a project to assess the attitudes, behaviors and value of the stakeholders regarding potential inclusion on the steering committee.

This is a tool that can be used to prevent the above scenario.

4.   Who is the Steering Committee Leader?

Who is the steering committee leader, and why were they given this responsibility? This is an important question to answer that will allow you to understand the culture of the organization.

Do keep in the back of your mind, in a political world, that the steering committee leader and the associated leadership team may have been put in these influential positions with the possibility they are expected to fail. The goal might be to create an exit plan for these individuals.

The other super important question is: Does the steering committee leader own the functional area being optimized or transformed? We know many of these projects have cross-functional impact, but there can still be a functional area where the project is focused.

If the steering committee leader is a long-term employee, they may have actually been the Architect of the process under optimization and transformation. This fact adds a lot to the political intrigue as this area could be "their baby." When you run into the situation where you have to tell them that "their baby is ugly," watch out for hostility and fireworks. This can be the "worst-case scenario."

If someone else on the steering committee has the ugly baby, that is bad enough. But when it is the leader, sparks and fireworks will fly. Defense mode will be deployed!!!!

If someone else on the steering committee has the ugly baby, that is bad enough. But when it is the leader, sparks and fireworks will fly. Defense mode will be deployed!!!!

Before we go any further into an ugly baby tangent, allow me to introduce what I consider a change management concept, called the five stages of grief.9 The five stages of grief are commonly felt when someone has experienced a loss such as a death, divorce, or loss of a job, etc. But you may be wondering, *what does that have to do with business process optimization and transformation?*

Only everything.

What I have found on business process optimization and transformation projects I have been a part of is that people go through the five stages of grief all the time. The executive sponsor, steering committee, project manager and project team can experience a variety of losses during the project.

Many times when a team and I have started getting past symptoms and exposing root cause(s), I have seen a wide variety of grieving take hold in the organization. Multiple instances and examples of grieving depend on the complexity of the optimization and transformation project. As I highlight the five stages of grief, you'll see they might occur in a project team as we go through the chapters.

Even before you get to root causes, which magnify grieving, you will find many instances where "reality sets in." When this happens, the project team and steering committee gain an understanding of how bad the situation is.

I bring this up here because if the steering committee leader's area is the one actually under optimization and transformation, you can face some interesting political challenges. They may be totally against the project and may have been forced into being the steering committee leader.

The five stages of grief are typically part of change management and manifest when the executive sponsor, steering committee, project leader and project team feel a sense of loss.

Dr. Elisabeth Kubler-Ross has identified the five stages of grief people go through following a serious loss.[10] Sometimes people get stuck in one of the first four stages. Their lives can be painful until they move onto the fifth stage: Acceptance.

"The Five Stages of Grief"

1. **Denial and Isolation.** At first, we tend to deny the loss has taken place and may withdraw from our usual social contacts. This stage may last a few moments or longer.

2. **Anger.** The grieving person may be furious at the person who inflicted the hurt, or they may be enraged at themselves or the world, for letting it happen. They may be angry with themselves for letting the event take place, even if, realistically, nothing could have stopped it.

3. **Bargaining.** Now, the grieving person may propose bargains, asking a higher power or other entity, for example, "If I do this, will you take away the loss?"

4. **Depression.**[1] The person feels numb, although anger and sadness may remain underneath.

5. **Acceptance.** Now, the anger, sadness and mourning have tapered off. The person simply accepts the reality of the loss."[11]

If you pay attention here, you can also pick up on a very important life lesson. Whether you have lost out on a great job opportunity or job, or if you have lost a parent or simply lost your golf swing, you will go through the five stages of grief.

When you hit the point where you realize that something has changed or will have to change, the five stages of grief kick in.

In business process optimization and transformation, you are always telling someone that something has to change.

Think about the situation when you have to tell an executive vice president (EVP), who is on the steering committee, that you have identified the root cause of the problem and that it is their area. The tension may grow as you elaborate on your recommendation for fixing it.

Think about the denial and anger you are going to face.

Huge!

---

1   "Depression" in this reference is intended to be interpreted as a broadly-used term that describes a feeling and does not denote a clinical diagnosis.

As the project leader, you need to know this is going to happen. How you navigate through the situation will be critical to success. This is the area where many optimization and transformation projects fail — because the root cause is so great and so overwhelming to fix — the organization can never work their way through to acceptance.

The organization will linger in depression. They will vacillate between the other four stages of grieving. Sure, they may make minor changes in the project as they are dealing with the five stages of grief, but the full requirements for optimization and transformation will stall. They will keep complaining about how screwed up the processes are. All because the executive sponsor and steering committee cannot get to the acceptance stage.

> **Because the root cause is so great and so overwhelming to fix, the organization can never work their way through to acceptance. The organization will linger in depression. They will vacillate between the other four stages of grieving.**

The Band-Aids® come out. The project ends, and the organization keeps doing what it does.

This is where your work as the Psychologist and Psychiatrist come in. It is critical you understand that you will face the five stages of grief in every project.

How you help navigate the executive sponsor, steering committee, project manager and project team to get to acceptance is a lot of painstaking work. If you are the project manager, you may say, "I did not sign up for this!"

Well, you did by default, and you better be prepared to handle the emotional rollercoaster of the five stages of grief. I have never been on an optimization or transformation project where I *did not* see the five stages of grief occur.

5.   Who is the Project Manager (PM)?

Who is the project manager, and why were they given this responsibility?

Project managers come in all shapes and forms.

- Experienced, inexperienced, sharp and not so sharp.

- Full of themselves, not full of themselves.

- Project Management Professional (PMP) or non-PMP-certified.

- The project manager will be your primary conduit on the project. *You* may be the project manager, so understand this role well.

The same questions that apply to the steering committee also apply to the project manager.

1.   Who are they and where do they fit into the organization?

2.   Are they a long-term employee or new hire?

As a long-term employee, they are embedded in the culture. As a new hire, they may not have developed their "network of influence." If a long-term employee, why were they put into the role of project manager? Have they shown previous success in managing projects? Are they an early-career leader being groomed or tested for advancement? Or are they a marginal player that upper management wants to remove from the organization, and this is the last hurrah?

You need to know and understand the project manager. If *you* are the project manager, you need to know why you were selected for the position.

A PMP-certified PM with business knowledge would be a nice package to lead the project!

I have also worked with great project managers who understood the business that did not have the PMP certification. They were very organized and very effective.

Companies wanting to groom early career professionals with PMP certification would be well suited to put the individual on a cross functional training program to expose them to a variety of aspects of the business. This cross functional training will only increase the value of the early career professional.

If you get or are the PM with the business knowledge, this can pose another problem. These types may very well own the area under optimization or transformation; they may have architected and managed the existing processes and have a vested interest in not looking bad.

I worked on one project where the project manager had owned the process under transformation for some time. He was a great guy, but as we decomposed the processes and drilled down to root causes, the PM got defensive and tried to derail some of the recommendations.

He hit the stages of grief *hard*.

Fortunately, other members of the project team were very strong A-Players, and they would not allow the project manager to derail fixing the root causes. The PM and members of the project team had a few heated, contentious discussions. They warned the PM they would escalate the issues up to the steering committee if he did not get on board.

After a few rounds of discussions, and some time to work through the stages of grief to acceptance, the PM finally came around to the task at hand, and that breakthrough is what transformed the broken processes.

You cannot underestimate how a PM may try to derail a project.

You cannot underestimate how a PM may try to derail a project.

As they periodically inform their boss about what is being found (note that their boss might be a direct line to the steering committee or one level removed), they can inadvertently derail the project if they, themselves, are in denial and starting the stages of grief. Emotions can get volatile and raw as these situations are taken personally. If you are the project manager, leave your prejudices at the door. Do what is right for the company, which is sometimes easier said than done.

Which leads us to our discussion on the project team.

6.   Who is on the project team?

We must first understand why the members were given this assignment.

Well, that depends on the optimization and transformation project.

One thing is for sure; you need some leaders on the project team who are A-Players.

As we'll have a broader discussion on change management later, let me take a few minutes here to talk about change champions.

What and who are change champions?

Change champions are well-respected and influential opinion leaders in the organization. They work well up and down the organizational charts as influencers. They are comfortable with uncertainty and ambiguity. They are good listeners and willing and eager to try new ideas and approaches. They value a knowledge-sharing culture and are strong participants in two-way conversations. Change champions come from across the organization depending on the project. They can come from accounting/finance, R&D, marketing, sales, supply chain, operations, etc.

Examples of change champions are the SMEs we discussed before from across the functional areas.

Your project team needs to have some strong change champions who are A-Players.

I want to discuss the change champion concept here because it is critical to get change champions on the project team. As we dive deeper into the role of change champions, let's not forget that change starts at the top of the organization.

As we dive deeper into the role of change champions, let's not forget that change starts at the top of the organization.

The executive sponsor and steering committee members are what I call executive change champions.

A few paragraphs ago, I talked about the project where the PM tried to derail some of the recommendations. This is where the change champions on the project team stepped in. They put their foot down and demanded that some of the more difficult recommendations be followed, or else it was all just a waste of time.

As I mentioned earlier, optimization and transformation projects allow for opportunities to test some of your "up-and-coming" managers and early-career leaders. This is also a good time to see if some of your "marginal" players can step up to the next level of maturity and performance.

I encountered exactly that situation on one of my projects.

The client had put two staff positions on the project team. These two staff members had worked for the company for a while. However, neither of the two had been particularly impactful in their previous jobs, but people still saw their potential.

After two weeks, I was not impressed by one of them and questioned one of the change champions about why that person was on the project. They were immature and did not seem to get the importance of being part of the team. I did not go to the project manager, but instead, wanted to see how the change champion would handle the situation.

I wondered: *will this person really evolve into the change champion they can be?*

Through some one-on-one counseling, the change champion explained to the team member how fortunate they were to be selected for the project, and that this was their time to shine. There would be no more complaining about being passed over for promotions if they grasped this opportunity and ran with it. The time was now or never.

Well, I will say I was impressed with the turnaround in the team member's attitude and performance. They became eager to participate and take on more responsibilities. They stepped up, and we could count on them to do very good work. *They* actually would mature into a change champion!

I was also very impressed with the change champion, who was able to light a fire under this person to get them moving in the right direction! That is what a change champion can do ... influence others to make the project a reality!

The point here is that the project team can be made up of a cross-section of the organization. At a minimum, you do need a few A-Players to be on the team. They are your initial change champions!

And one final note, make sure you have a representative from accounting/finance on the team as part of your change champion network. Many project decisions will come down to spending money. You want the change champion money person on your team to have been part of building the solution. They can clearly articulate to the steering committee the need for the level of financing you are asking the company to invest!

Organizational Culture

I will not profess to be an expert on organizational culture and what makes a good vs. bad culture, but it is important to know what kind of culture you are facing on the project.

A lot of research into organizational culture has been conducted. Books have been published, and papers written. I will highlight one perspective on organizational culture that I found appropriate for the purpose of this book.

Robert E. Quinn and Kim S. Cameron are professors at the University of Michigan. Quinn and Cameron developed the Organizational Culture Assessment Instrument (OCAI)[12], a validated survey method to assess current and preferred organizational cultures. The OCAI is based on Quinn and Cameron's Competing Values Framework Model.[13]

To determine what type of organizational culture you are working with, here is a summary of the four types and their specific qualities:

- ## The Clan Culture

   This culture is rooted in collaboration. Members share commonalities and see themselves as part of one big family who is active and involved. Leadership takes the form of mentorship, and the organization is bound by commitments and traditions.

   The main values are rooted in teamwork, communication and consensus. A prominent clan culture is Tom's of Maine[14], the maker of all-natural hygiene products. To create the brand, founder Tom Chappell focused on building respectful relationships with employees, customers, suppliers and the environment itself.

• The Adhocracy Culture

This culture is based on energy and creativity. Employees are encouraged to take risks, and leaders are seen as innovators or entrepreneurs. The organization is held together by experimentation, with an emphasis on individual ingenuity and freedom.

The core values are based on change and agility. Amazon and Google can be seen as a prototypical adhocracy organization. Jeff Bezos, Larry Page and Sergey Brin are the consummate innovators and entrepreneurs.

• The Market Culture

This culture is built upon the dynamics of competition and achieving concrete results. The focus is goal-oriented, with leaders who are tough and demanding. The organization is united by a common goal to succeed and beat all rivals.

The main value drivers are market share and profitability. The old General Electric (G.E.) under ex-CEO Jack Welch[15] is a good example of this culture. Welch vowed that every G.E. business unit must rank first or second in its respective market or face being sold off. Another example of market culture is software giant Oracle under hard-driving Executive Chairman Larry Ellison.[16] Note: I worked at Oracle during the Go Go Internet Days. Believe me when I say it was tough and demanding but also exhilarating.

• The Hierarchy Culture

This culture is founded on structure and control. The work environment is formal, with strict institutional procedures in place for guidance. Leadership is based on organized coordination and monitoring, with a culture emphasizing efficiency and predictability.

The values include consistency and uniformity. Think of stereotypical large, bureaucratic organizations[17] – the military, or the Department of Motor Vehicles or Apple. Yes, I believe Apple has moved from an Adhocracy to a Hierarchy culture.

Why is it important to know the culture of the organization, anyway?

It ties back to our work as an Anthropologist.

I am an **Anthropologist**, studying various aspects of organizational behavior within past and present. I research topics that include the discovery of norms that explore the social and cultural DNA of the organization.

How can you manage a large optimization or transformation project without knowing the culture, how the organization behaves, and what the cultural norms are that define decision making?

If it is an internal project you are managing, which of the four cultures you just learned about best describes your organization?

Next, ask: where has the organization been and where are they today?

Did the board bring in a new CEO to move from the hierarchy culture to the adhocracy culture or the clan culture to the market culture?

A Case of Culture

I worked on a project where the new CEO was tasked to change the culture of the organization from a hierarchy culture to an adhocracy culture.

I worked on a project where the new CEO was tasked to change the culture of the organization from a hierarchy culture to an adhocracy culture.

Wow, was that an interesting one ...

The hierarchy team vs. the adhocracy team were working to sustain dominance. The hierarchy team was rooted in their ways, as any good hierarchy team would be and saw no need to adopt the adhocracy team approach to running the business. The CEO did not appreciate what it took to change the culture of the organization.

One might ask *how hard it is to get people to change when they do not want to change?*

When I first started working, I was given advice on how to hire my team. My boss was an experienced corporate warrior nearing retirement age. He was a great guy and an early mentor but not for long, unfortunately.

We were having lunch out of the office on a Friday at noon. Back in the day, you could go out for lunch, drink a few beers, and maybe get back to the office around 3:00 p.m. Well, after a couple of beers, my boss got a bit philosophical.

He said, "Dave, this will be one of the most important pieces of advice anyone will give you in your work life. Only hire people you have to reel in vs. kicking them in the ass. Meaning, reeling in aggressive people is much easier than having to kick a lazy person in the ass to get the work done. Do this and your life as a manager, and leader will be a lot less complicated."

This is not to say that people in the hierarchy culture are lazy; they just operate at a different level of urgency vs. the adhocracy culture.

Well, after over a year of dealing with the hierarchy team, the CEO finally realized, with some help from outside consultants, that they needed to make some changes on the leadership team replacing hierarchy leaders with adhocracy leaders.

After that change, the leadership was made up of all adhocracy leaders. The new leaders came in and instilled the level of urgency that was missing. As I mentioned before, change happens from the top of the organization down. But leaders also have to be open to change.

There were some casualties of hierarchy personnel leaving, but that turned out to be a good thing. They would not be happy in the adhocracy culture anyway. And some of the hierarchy team stepped up and became part of the adhocracy team. *They* found it to be exciting!

I have worked with Fortune 50, Fortune 100, and smaller companies you have never heard of.

You can't assume you know a company's culture before you arrive. And you need the answer to, what is your litmus test as an internal employee?

The size of the organization and the complexity of it don't matter.

One of the first things I do when I start a project is to meet with the leadership team/steering committee to ask questions about the project and also, most importantly, questions about their culture and how decisions are made.

> 🔍 **You can't assume you know a company's culture before you arrive. And you need the answer to, what is your litmus test as an internal employee?**

You will be surprised that in many cases, my presumed understanding of their culture was different than what the leadership team/steering committee articulated.

Even more surprising, different opinions prevailed amongst the leadership team/steering committee on the company culture. This has happened only occasionally, but it has happened.

So, try not to be surprised if you encounter it.

If you are working on an internal optimization or transformation project, as strange as it seems, ask the executive sponsor and leadership team/steering committee, "How would you define our corporate culture?"

My team started a huge transformation project with a Fortune 50 company. Everyone said how difficult it was to work with this company and how challenging our project was going to be to make the changes necessary for the transformation. What we found was interesting.

At first, the client was loud, waving their hands, saying that it was their way or the highway. Over a short period, as we were explaining what was going to happen in the transformation project, a strange turn happened. They became much less boisterous and loud, and — hard to imagine — somewhat passive. They were positively a hierarchy culture.

How did this happen?

As our team showed them that we knew more about aspects of their business challenges than they did and that we could support our positions with fact-based analysis, we were now working from a position as a Trusted Advisor.

Were there road bumps along the way? Of course, but overall, the journey was not what we expected based on perceived knowledge of their culture.

I remember in one particular meeting; we presented solid analysis that even surprised us as to what we found (Archaeologist). We were about halfway through the presentation when the head of the steering committee asked us a simple question. "How can you and your team in two months, uncover this much knowledge when we for years could not put our finger on what was going on?" Well, the answer *was* simple and a bit arrogant, I will say in hindsight. But I remarked, "That's exactly why you hired us!"

This was a pivotal moment of establishing our credibility.

After this moment, the head of the steering committee could clearly understand the value of bringing in someone from the outside to see their organization from a different set of lenses.

From that day forward, we enhanced our position as trusted advisors because we had established structure and control within a formal work environment with procedures in place to best benefit our project.

The hierarchy culture loved the discipline!

Note: If I can make one point and *this is huge*, never, and I mean never, get in the position where you and the team have significantly fallen behind and the steering committee feels they have to dig into your daily activities. If this is an internal project, and you are the project manager, never let your internal teams drag you behind. You and your project team must lead and set the direction. You need to keep your positions as the trusted advisor because, once trust is lost, it is hard to get it back.

Never, and I mean never, get in the position where you and the team have significantly fallen behind and the steering committee feels they have to dig into your daily activities.

A big part of solving mysteries is understanding the makeup of the organization and its culture.

You must be able to answer:

1. Is the executive sponsor an insider, or outsider?
2. What is the makeup of the steering committee — are they insiders or outsiders?
3. Who is the steering committee leader? Are they an insider, or outsider?
4. Is the organization a: clan, hierarchy, adhocracy, or market culture?

All this knowledge we glean as the Anthropologist helps us to understand how we have to deal with the executive sponsor, steering committee, project manager and project team.

If you are the project manager for an internal project, get familiar with these concepts and how you have seen them work in the past. Do they validate your assumptions about your organization?

Subcultures

We have spent a good amount of time discussing the culture of an organization. But what about the subcultures that exist within an organization.

Subcultures? Yes, subcultures.

Using the same four cultures, think about the cultures of:

- Executive Suite
- Research & Development
- Marketing
- Sales
- Supply Chain
- Operations
- Regulatory
- Finance
- Information Technology

Each one of these "departments" may exhibit their own unique cultures within the broader culture of the organization.

This is where we see the issues with silos being developed, where communications between the departments is strained because their department cultures clash.

Each department may adhere to the overall company culture, but they each can operate independently of the company culture with their own subculture.

In our example of Adhocracy vs. Hierarchy culture the CEO was trying to instill, it was R&D and marketing vs. supply chain and operations.

R&D and marketing were Adhocracy and supply chain and operations were Hierarchy.

The Sales Department also had an Adhocracy culture.

The wild card was finance, who had a Market culture, tough and demanding.

The only culture missing in the organization was the Clan culture.

So, who do you think finance usually sided with? Adhocracy for sure.

Adhocracy and Market cultures get along much better with each other than with the Hierarchy.

Culture Summary

When looking to understand a company's culture, look to understand the overall company culture but make sure you understand the subcultures of each department.

It will give you insights into how the Silos are designed and how these departments will interact with each other when you face cross functional solutions to solving the mystery.

There's one final takeaway for this chapter: Think about the five stages of grief as they have occurred — in your life or in the projects you have been involved with. You are going to encounter them, so be prepared.

CHAPTER 4

BUSINESS PROCESSES

Thomas Davenport defines a business process as "a structured, measured set of activities designed to produce a specific output for a particular customer or market. It implies a strong emphasis on how work is done within an organization. A process is thus a specific ordering of work activities across time and space, with a beginning and an end, and clearly defined inputs and outputs, a structure for action. Processes are the structure by which an organization does what is necessary to produce value for its customers."[18]

Could not have said it better myself.

Although there are a number of moving parts in business process optimization and transformation, it ultimately gets down to the process. Everything supports the process.

As a Six Sigma Black Belt, one of the most important concepts of the training states that: Over time, every process will break down unless a continuous improvement approach is taken to regularly improve the process.

Well, that just does not happen in most companies.

What usually happens is that a process is created; it morphs over time to a different process – in many cases, a more complicated process – and nobody pays any attention to the process as it evolves.

Without deliberate and regular process management reviews, business processes evolve in uncoordinated ways with unintended consequences.

This results in suboptimal and even dysfunctional business processes.

Take a new process when an Enterprise Resource Planning (ERP) system or other technology system is implemented. The consultant may use what in the industry is called a "best practice." This approach is usually elected to save time and money on the implementation. Best practices are typically very straightforward and not overly complicated.

Over time as the organization uses the new ERP system, they will find that best practices may not meet all their business requirements.

The company starts making business process changes to meet their business requirements.

In many cases, the process changes are done outside of the ERP system's capabilities as the company does not want to spend more money on system enhancements and upgrades.

They would rather add manual processes that often are supported by Excel.

This means the idea of "one version of the truth" is compromised.

Before I get ahead of myself, let me explain what I mean.

One version of the truth is the ideal of having a single, centralized repository which stores all of an organization's data to ensure consistent analysis and reporting.

The single repository of data is designed to prevent employees from showing up at meetings with multiple Excel workbooks and no matching data!

When the process evolves to where the left hand does not know what the right hand is doing and this continues over a number of years, you get a mixed bag of systems and manual processes.

Of course, it is likely that no one has ever *documented* the changing process.

Cracks develop in the efficiency of the process as more and more people are added to the process, each with their own manual process.

What you find and this is part of Six Sigma training, is that processes break down most significantly where the handoff of the process occurs.

Meaning you now have a wide variety of manual processes, many based on Excel records with multiple handoffs occurring throughout the process.

And *again*, nothing is documented.

Does this sound familiar? It should. If it doesn't, then I am surprised.

This story is played over and over again across most companies, in most processes, in most industries, and across the world. Large companies, small companies, mid-size companies, it does not matter; we see this breakdown over and over again.

I have seen this business phenomenon in R&D, marketing, regulatory, sales, supply chain, operations, finance and IT. In fact, there is no place I have not seen this business phenomenon.

Solving the mysteries of the processes is what I consider the most interesting part of business process optimization and transformation. It is these mysteries that get me out of bed every day with excitement and energy.

We'll now discuss "the process" we'll use to solve the mysteries of the process.

Current State Process Documentation

I personally believe that documenting the current state business process is the most important part of a business process optimization and transformation program.

Yes, we do have to develop the future state processes to move the optimization or transformation forward, but without getting the correct state processes documented and flushed out, you cannot find the true root causes of the problem.

I've changed my opinion here a bit. I used to believe we could just jump the organization to the future state processes. I now believe you really need to start with documenting current state processes.

I worked on projects where we went straight to future state design because the existing technology or processes were so bad.

But I learned that we missed out on opportunities to get a better understanding of the organization as a whole. We missed out on the opportunities to get to know the people, the culture and the real problems.

Documenting the current state processes gives you an opportunity to work with the people of the organization, and to understand how they think, and problem solve.

What is the craziness they are dealing with in their everyday jobs?

Why is this process so broken?

You will experience a lot of "aha" moments when undertaking current state process documentation.

When documenting the current state process, you are using your skills as the Archaeologist, Anthropologist, Detective and Psychologist to truly understand what is going on in the process and company.

Some business processes can be very complicated.

Let's look at a new product introduction/development (NPID) process with all the cross-functional teams involved.

The NPID process is complicated and can span a number of months or even years as well as it can be global in nature.

I'll try to provide a good example using a stage-gate process.

A stage-gate process is a project management technique where a project is divided into distinct stages, separated by decision points known as gates.[19]

A stage-gate process usually governs the NPID Process.

At each gate, a steering committee or governance board (executive team) decides project continuation.

The decision is made on forecasts and information available at the time, including the business case, risk analysis and availability of necessary resources, such as personnel, technology and investment dollars.

Different parts of the business come into the project as the project progresses through the different gates.

Depending on the complexity of the project and how the organization views projects, you can have anywhere from 3-5 gates.

Let's take a look at the NPID process in a 3-stage, stage-gate model for a consumer packaged-goods (CPG) company.

New Product Introduction (NPID)

As you can see, introducing a new product requires a true cross-functional effort.

You will also see that there are many sub-processes within the overall NPID process.

In this example, the process may span multiple countries where participants are scattered around the globe.

It's ultra-complex when you are looking at cross-functional teams around the world.

Processes come in all shapes and sizes from simple, to complex to ultra-complex.

Examples

Let's review a few examples of process optimization and transformation. As mentioned previously, here are a few definitions.

Optimization: An act, process, or methodology of making something (such as a design, system, or decision) as fully perfect, functional, or effective as possible.

Transformation: A change of variables in which a function of new variables is substituted for original variables, which results in a change of composition.

Art: Something that is created with imagination and skill, and that is beautiful, or that expresses important ideas or feelings.

Science: A systematic enterprise that builds and organizes knowledge in the form of testable explanations and predictions about the universe.[20]

When optimizing a process, the goal is to maximize the efficiency and effectiveness of one or more of the process steps or activities.

When transforming a process, the goal is to implement approaches and methods that are a substitute for old processes with the aim of the new processes being to bring fresh levels of efficiency and effectiveness.

Process optimization and transformation requires you to create with imagination and skill!

Process optimization and transformation is as much an art as it is a science.

Process optimization and transformation is as much an art as it is a science.

What I have found over my career in process optimization and transformation is that any business discipline is a candidate for process optimization and transformation whether accounting, sales and marketing, supply chain, manufacturing operations, information technology, regulatory, etc.

Why is this?

As you learn in Six Sigma Black Belt training, any process will deteriorate over time if no continuous improvement plan is applied to the process. In most cases, organizations establish a process, let it evolve and then ultimately, it deteriorates because there is no process monitoring, and no continuous improvement plans have been put into place.

To give you an idea of just a few examples of process optimization and transformation projects where I have been solving mysteries,

I will review four projects: "My First Mystery," "A Continuing Mystery," "A Global Mystery" and "A Mega Mystery."

MY FIRST MYSTERY, SOLVED!

My first exposure to business process optimization came early in my career when I was a plant cost accountant. I was sent to a plant which had profitability problems.

They were losing money each and every month, and this had been the case for a while.

The management team could not identify what was going wrong because it was not one single issue; the entire end-to-end process was affected.

It was a composite of multiple, independent but integrated processes.

I performed what we called post-production analysis (PPA). PPA was a forensic analysis (Archaeologist) that looks at the life of a customer order, known today as a "Day In the Life Study" (DILO). We'll discuss DILO in more detail in a later chapter.

Post-production analysis is a bit deceiving as the analysis followed the end-to-end process of an order from customer service (quote) through production.

These were the core, integrated business processes for this custom manufacturing operation.

No one had reviewed the integrated end-to-end processes resulting in an incomplete picture. Many cause and effect relationships are associated with every stage from quoting an order to getting it out the door.

The review encompassed a random selection of orders run through the plant over the previous 6-month period. The following are the results from the PPA.

Customer Service

During this period of time, there was a lot of volatility in the raw materials' markets, the volatility being that the raw material prices were going mostly up.

Each custom order was costed and priced by a customer service representative based on a variety of raw materials, manufacturing costs and overhead allocations supplied by plant accounting.

After developing fully loaded costs, an "A, B, C" selling price was supplied to the salesperson. The highest commission for sales was the "A" price with diminishing commissions for "B and C."

Salespeople were not authorized to sell below the "C" price level. Below "C" required approval from the regional VP of Sales.

Typically a 60–90-day delay elapsed from when orders were quoted to customers until orders were placed and run through the plant. In a number of cases, the quotes were good for an entire year.

FINDINGS

Raw Materials

As raw materials escalated during this time period, the actual acquisition costs for raw materials for production was greater than the raw material costs on the quotes — reducing margins significantly.

Production

Production was a multi-stage process utilizing a machine hour rate for each process: setup/change time, run rate/hour and teardown time.

A variety of setup/change times, run rates and teardown times were used based on the product being produced.

Yield and waste factors were also applied to the cost basis, which was applicable to the product being produced.

A variety of issues were identified.

The actual setup/change times were longer than the quoted setup/change times. In a number of cases, they were off by 50%. As an example, the actual setup/change time was three hours vs. a one and half hour estimated setup/change time.

An undocumented element of the setup/change issue was that certain items took longer to set up based on the previous product being produced.

Meaning, the sequencing of different products through the production process could have an adverse effect on the setup/change times for subsequent products.

If product X ran after product J, then the setup/change time for product X was accurate. But if product X ran after product Q, then the setup/change time for product X took twice as long. Each setup/change was looked at as an independent event when in actuality, there was a cause and effect relationship between what was produced previously on the production line.

This next item was significant.

The actual items produced per hour on the machines were in some cases, 30% below the quoted production rate. For instance, the standard production rate quoted was 40 items per hour, but the actual production rate was 28 items per hour, a 30% error factor.

This translated to a production run of 500 items estimated to take 12.5 hours. At a machine hour rate of say $200, that equates to an estimated production cost of $2,500. In actuality, the 500 items took 17.9 hours at 28 items per hour. The actual cost of production was $3,580 vs. the estimate of $2,500 for a production loss of $1,080.

Quotes were predicated off standard production rates. But the standard production rates had not been updated and validated in years. Quotes underestimated the actual production costs, in this example by 30%

On top of that, the actual yield on raw materials was down between 10-15 % over the quoted yield.

For example, 100 lbs. of raw materials were expected to yield 75 units of finished product. The actual yield was 68 units of finished product from 100 lbs. of raw materials. If the raw material was $5/lb., then 100 lbs. would cost $500. Instead of an estimated cost of $6.66/unit, the cost was actually $7.35/unit.

Sales Orders

For a number of the selected sales orders, The "A, B, C" pricing model was abandoned due to a "competitive situation" and quotes were priced at or below break-even costs.

Case Conclusion

Actual raw material costs were higher than quoted raw material costs during the production time.

Longer setup/change times, lower yields and slower production rates caused actual production costs to be much higher than quoted production costs.

Pricing "at or below" break-even cause the orders to be priced at a loss because the cost basis for break-even was understated. **In other words, the more we sold, the more we lost!**

It is hopefully obvious that there were a number of contributors to the breakdown of the process. However, it should be noted that one item by itself was significant enough. When you bring all the issues to light, in a comprehensive end-to-end integrated review, you can see the magnitude of the problem.

The Five Stages of Grief

At this point in my life, I had never heard of the Five Stages of Grief. That would come many, many years later.

I was very nervous for the initial meeting with the regional General Manager, VP of Sales, Plant Manager and my boss, the Plant Accountant, where I was to present my findings.

I observed the first stage of grief —denial — in this meeting.

The General Manager, VP of Sales and Plant Manager progressively got the "deer in the headlight" look as I was explaining the details of what I had found. They all appeared frozen in denial. The VP of Sales, a usually very boisterous guy, was very quiet.

After they got over their initial shock, they started asking questions, challenging my findings.

My boss did a great job preparing me for the meeting so I had all my ducks in a row and was able to explain my findings in detail. My boss had my back and did a great job supporting me.

During their questioning, I could see their eyes dart back and forth amongst themselves, as the possible reality of the situation may have been starting to creep in.

The regional General Manager kept staring at me. My boss later told me that after I left the meeting, he was very angry (the second stage of grief). He asked no one in particular and maybe even himself, "How could this kid find out this information because we've been totally lost as to what the hell has been going on?"

At the anger stage, when mysteries have been identified, many times the anger is self-directed internally. This was the case here. The GM was angry at himself, first and foremost.

Then he got angry at everyone else.

The next day, there was some negotiating — the third stage of grief — as they had me sit down with the Production Manager and go through my findings in detail to validate what I had uncovered.

He asked me on more than one occasion why I didn't come to him first with what I was finding. I explained to him that my role was as an auditor, and that I had to keep my findings confidential. I could not let the proverbial cat out of the bag.

The regional GM was an action leader, so there was little time for depression. He got the team moving fast to acceptance and onto our corrective action plan.

Corrective Action

1. Plant accounting started to supply cost updates monthly vs. quarterly.
2. The quote to order time was reduced to 45 days.
3. A quarterly pricing review was inserted into yearly sales contracts.
4. Setup/change times, yields and production rates were updated to reflect actual history every 12 months, with a six-month review for validation.
5. Continuous improvement projects were kicked off to improve setup/change times, yields and production rates.
6. 5% above break-even costs were the lowest-allowed selling price and only with the approval of the regional VP of sales and the regional general manager.

Results

Within six months, we had turned the plant around to profitability.

When we closed the books for the first time with a profit in such a short period of time, the general feeling was "no way!"

We booked the profit to a reserve account and reported break-even results to the corporate office.

This was a great improvement from the losses, so the corporate team was pleased to see the progress.

The next month we showed another profit and released some profits from the reserve account.

The third month we showed stronger profits and released more of the reserve account.

Over a total of six months, we released all the reserve profits.

While I was at the plant, we never reported another loss. After the third month, we started having monthly "profit parties" at a local restaurant.

I had solved my first mystery!!!!!!!!!!!!!!!

A Continuing Mystery

This is a story about creating an early-stage Sales & Operations Planning (S&OP) model.

S&OP is an integrated business management process led by the executive team which continually achieves focus, alignment and synchronization among all functions of the organization.

The S&OP process includes monthly updated forecasts for the sales plan, supply and distribution plan, production plan, inventory plan and new product development plan along with the strategic initiative plan and resultant financial plans.

A properly implemented S&OP process routinely reviews demand and supply resources and plans out 18+ months across this rolling time horizon.

S&OP has evolved into a major business process. A new S&OP implementation is a significant transformation project.

It is one of the most critical business processes used to achieve best-in-class performance to outperform competitors consistently.

I had recently been promoted to the position of materials manager (from assistant controller/cost accounting manager) and was tasked to consolidate the supply chain management of four separate business divisions into a consolidated supply chain management organization.

The four divisions had manufacturing and distribution facilities across the Continental United States, Alaska and the Caribbean.

The four divisions were quite distinct, with very different product lines and customer bases.

Thus, there was a wide variety of raw materials, suppliers, production facilities, distribution needs and delivery requirements.

Our "operations" organization took on the responsibilities for demand and production planning, purchasing, logistics and customer service.

Demand planning at the time was a very new concept.

If you are not familiar with demand planning, it is the process of forecasting the demand for a product or service, so it can be produced and delivered more efficiently and to the satisfaction of customer demands.

We'll start on how we transformed the supply chain planning function for the largest division, which was also the most broken.

When you look at optimization or transformation projects, you need to be able to differentiate between "symptoms" vs. "root causes" to the problem(s).

One common mode failure for unsuccessful process optimization and transformation projects is that the teams focus on fixing the symptoms and not the root causes.

The teams chase their tail fixing symptoms, don't understand the "cause and effect relationships" between the symptoms and the root causes.

We'll go into more detail on symptoms and root causes in a later chapter.

The symptoms for this division were very evident once we started looking at the problems.

1. 3 – 5 pages of delayed orders/backorders
2. Trouble meeting "first-time quality" in production
3. Constant changes to the production schedules
4. Raw material shortages
5. High inventory levels
6. Excessive demurrage charges
7. Expedited inbound and outbound freight
8. Excessive overtime
9. Volatile manufacturing costs

I lead our cross-functional transformation team (materials, customer service, purchasing and plant management) in the analysis by asking a constant stream of "whys."

I would later learn about the 5 Whys in Six Sigma Black Belt Training. As I mentioned before, a number of concepts in the advanced methodologies (such as Six Sigma) were work we were doing previously but were not a defined specific approach. Asking questions and why relates to common sense to solving a problem or mystery.

We'll go into more detail on the 5 Whys in a later chapter.

1. Why do we have so many delayed orders?
2. Why do we have "first-time quality" issues?
3. Why do we constantly change production schedules?
4. Why are we out of critical, regular raw materials?
5. Why are our inventory levels so high, and why did we have raw material shortages?
6. Why do we have all these demurrage charges?
7. Why do we have all these expedited freight shipments?
8. Why do we have such high overtime in the plants?
9. Why are our manufacturing costs so volatile?

Case Conclusion

As we worked through the analysis, and the answers to our questions, the root cause of these issues became very apparent.

The issue could all be traced back to a singular root cause: planning!

Our demand planning processes were nonexistent.

Production planning was based on "Which customer is screaming the loudest this week or today?"

As an operational accountant moving into materials management, I was familiar with developing budgets, and monthly monitoring actuals vs. plan and quarterly updates to budgets.

To me, the concepts of demand planning and production planning were very similar to budgeting and planning in finance.

This is how we started the demand planning, using financial planning techniques.

To breakdown our findings further, there was a significant cause and effect relationship between planning and:

1. Delayed orders/backorders
2. First-time quality
3. Changing production schedules
4. Raw material shortages
5. High inventory levels
6. Excessive demurrage charges
7. Excessive expedited freight
8. Excessive plant overtime
9. Volatile manufacturing costs

The Five Stages of Grief

I don't remember us going through the five stage of grief on this transformation project. We were in such bad shape, there was no time for grieving. We were at acceptance right away. The only question was whether we could pull it off and we did.

Corrective Action

We transformed our planning processes by implementing demand planning, along with future looking production planning.

Demand planning is an essential step in supply chain planning.

For make-to-stock products, our demand planning at the time involved simple statistical planning where we looked at the history and then the forecast of our future demand.

For make-to-order products, we used the actual delivery dates to incorporate into our demand plan.

We provided a make-to-order product lead time to the sales department so they could communicate the lead times to our customers.

At this time in supply chain management, the buzz was material requirement planning (MRP), not demand planning.

My question when I went to an MRP class was: "How can you plan for materials before you plan for demand?"

That question was not answered.

We moved to a process where the production planning for the plants was based on our demand plans.

It's interesting to note these are the core leading practices in supply chain management and S&OP today.

We developed the demand planning and production planning methodology and processes many years before they were commonly used.

We started relatively simply but created a huge impact. We forecasted the demand out to 16 weeks.

This was a huge change!

From the demand plans, we developed production plans for weeks 2-16.

Weeks 8-16 covered mid-term planning, weeks 5-8 were pretty solid, and weeks 1-4 were very tight.

The final production plans detailed scheduling for the coming week and were created by the plants.

We implemented bi-weekly planning meetings where we would review the demand plans and production plans.

We implemented a weekly meeting on Fridays, where we would review the detailed schedules for the coming week.

We set aggressive KPI targets to:

1. Eliminate delayed orders
2. Improve first-time quality
3. Minimize production schedule changes
4. Eliminate raw material shortages
5. Reduce inventory levels
6. Eliminate demurrage charge
7. Eliminate expedited freight
8. Eliminate plant overtime
9. Eliminate volatile manufacturing costs

We intuitively looked at forecast accuracy as it was not a common KPI at the time. If the plants ran well and we met the eight KPIs we had established, then we must have been doing well with forecast accuracy.

Forecast bias was also measured intuitively. Forecast bias was not a common KPI at the time. If we weren't filling the warehouses up with product and we weren't delaying shipments, then we must have been doing well with forecast bias.

Forecast accuracy and forecast bias are the two major metrics when evaluating your performance in demand planning.

Forecast accuracy determines if the estimate you have made regarding customer(s) demand for a product (s) is correct.

Accurately predicting customer demand is critical to the supply chain when manufacturers are looking to optimize manufacturing efficiencies, inventory levels and avoid out of stock situations.

Forecast bias determines whether you are too high or too low with your forecast.

A high forecast bias means you are over-forecasting demand, which will lead to excess inventories and possibly over-capacity in the manufacturing plants.

A low forecast bias will lead to inadequate inventories and out-of-stock situations. It could lead to the manufacturing plants always cutting into production runs with inefficient plant utilization trying to play catch up with out-of-stock orders.

Results

Of course, we had some fits and starts along the way, but we had a committed team and great support from our executive leadership.

The results were astounding.

Within three months, we felt we had the planning processes and the plants under control and were headed in the right direction.

Within six months, we were in full operations mode, accelerating the changes we were seeking.

Within a year, we had moved the planning horizons out to six months.

Within a year and a half, we had implemented this early stage of S&OP model across all four business divisions with outstanding results.

Our KPI Target Results:

1. Eliminate delayed orders/backorders — reduced to a handful of orders

2. Improve first-time quality — occasional quality incident

3. Minimize production schedule changes — only for emergency situations

4. Eliminate raw material shortages – no raw material shortages

5. Reduce inventory levels – inventory levels dropped by 20%

6. Eliminate demurrage charges – occasional demurrage charge

7. Eliminate expedited freight – occasional expedited freight

8. Eliminate plant overtime – little to no overtime

9. Eliminate volatile manufacturing costs – stabilized manufacturing costs

We significantly exceeded the results for all of our KPIs.

I'll share two interesting (to me) stories from our transformation in S&OP.

Story #1

In one of our weekly planning meetings, we were getting into it a bit with one of the plant managers about a few changes to the weekly detailed schedule.

I was pressing him pretty hard about why the changes had to be made.

After a somewhat heated exchange, the plant manager asked for a time out.

He then composed himself and stated to the team and me, "Look, this is my job to run the plant and your team's job to handle the planning. Let me run the plant because that is what I was hired to do. And if I screw up, you can jump all over me and have my ass. But until then, you have got to trust me that I am making the right decisions."

Well, how could you argue with that! *Go for it, bro*! And he did!

We never had that conversation again because he and his team did a great job running the plant.

Story #2

This story involves how our new planning system affected our relationship with one of our most critical suppliers. This supplier was where we were experiencing a lot of expedited freight to get their materials to our plant. The cost of expedited freight was killing us financially. (Did I mention I hated expedited freight!?)

We were about four months into the transformation when we were awarded a large government contract.

Large government contracts traditionally brought the plants to their knees, but we were prepared this time.

We developed our demand and production plans out over multiple months to cover the contract and evaluated our raw material requirements (MRP).

After we had determined our raw material requirements, we set up a planning session with the supplier.

We laid out our requirements week by week for the raw material and emphasized that there were to be "no expedited shipments" as we were giving them ample time to plan their production.

Well, the supplier's team was flabbergasted.

They had never received a material requirement plan as we'd just laid out.

They were ecstatic and said that we had just changed our relationship.

Meeting our supply requirements would be no problem.

Low and behold, they came back to us a week later with a price reduction for the raw material in question.

They said that by giving them such a great material requirements plan, they could run their plant more efficiently. So, they wanted to share some of the savings with us!

Thank you very much.

We moved from expedited trucks racing across the country to railcars delivering the raw material to meet our production schedules.

Think early stage "just in time" (JIT) inventory. JIT is an inventory strategy where materials are ordered and received to align to when they are specifically needed. It is a Lean strategy to minimize inventories to improve the management of working capital.

What we had set up was an early-stage S&OP program.

Transforming the way in which we planned brought us closer to other departments in the company as we were removing silos.

We coordinated discussions with R&D on new product introductions/development (NPID) and material changes.

We held a monthly sales meeting to review our demand plans.

Our purchasing team negotiated better pricing on our raw materials.

We established inventory targets and financial models for raw materials and finished goods.

We reviewed with our executive team important supply chain decisions.

We created a performance management system with KPIs to manage our continuous improvement goals.

The methodology we put into place would now be called S&OP.

So, why do I call this story a "Continuing Mystery?"

I started this early stage model of S&OP actually a few decades ago.

Yes, a few decades ago.

There was no name for what we were creating. We did not give it a name.

As I have mentioned before, consultants came up with names, in this case, S&OP.

Of course, the model has matured considerably over the years; the more advanced model of S&OP is now Integrated Business Planning (IBP).

When I say a "Continuing Mystery," it is because I have implemented multiple S&OP programs over the last five years.

The concept and model of S&OP is still a revelation to clients!

I continually have to "educate" clients as to the structure of the S&OP methodology and what are the derived benefits!

I am mystified that S&OP and now IBP is still not as well understood as I would think after all these years.

And it's not small companies I am talking about; it's multi-billion-dollar companies.

I believe that it is now time that we consider sunsetting S&OP as it is a methodology. S&OP has been around for 40 years.

Integrated Business Planning has been around for 20 years, so the methodology is not new. IBP should now be the de facto standard for Enterprise Planning.

And, I believe we will see very soon the emergence of Automated Business Planning, ABP, which will be based on Artificial Intelligence, Machine Learning, Robotic Process Automation and Prescriptive Analytics. I coined the term ABP. I'm not sure if ABP will stick, but I do believe the future of Enterprise Planning will be based on Artificial Intelligence, Machine Learning, Robotic Process Automation and Prescriptive Analytics.

A GLOBAL MYSTERY

I find this next process optimization project interesting because it highlights that the opportunities for process optimization can be found in many, many, many corporate functions.

The optimization was phase one of an optimization and transformation roadmap that we built with the client. I will discuss the optimization project.

Global regulatory compliance describes the management system organizations must have in place to ensure that they are aware of and have implemented the proper process controls to comply with relevant international and local laws, policies and regulations.

Global regulations have increased significantly over the past decade or two resulting in the need for greater operational transparency.

Global organizations, in particular, have been required to increase the adoption of consolidated and harmonized sets of compliance processes and controls.

This client is one of the top energy companies in the world. With revenues in excess of $300 billion, 80,000+ employees and operations in 80 countries, this is one behemoth of an organization.

Our technology company had implemented a software platform that was used to create and manage complex regulatory documents around the globe for this client.

This was very sophisticated in nature due to a mix of global regulations. The client company employed a team of 80 regulatory professionals in two locations to manage the more than one million documents produced annually in 37 languages and 13 different formats.

To say this was a bit complex is an understatement.

As we have learned, any process left unattended or uncontrolled will deteriorate over time.

And this was the opposite case here.

Over a 5-year period, after the initial software implementation, more than 1,000 customizations were added to the system, with another 50 slated for development and 300 bug fixes to come.

The software and processes deteriorated because of all of the customization. The software and processes were not unattended; they were over-attended and out of control.

This was our biggest and worst client, which made the urgency that much more critical.

I had joined our company as VP of Services, and my #1 priority was to get this very critical client and our solution back on track.

At about the same time, the client transferred a mid-career leader from another part of the company who had developed a reputation as a problem solver to figure out what the heck was going on.

When meeting with the client management team for the first time, it became apparent that we, the solution provider, were considered to be the problem and they, the client, were reluctant participants of the circumstances at hand.

There was a lot of anger, frustration and hostility.

Usually in these situations, the supplier is the problem. This was the case here. We were the problem; they had nothing to do with the complex mess that had been created.

You can only guess how this story will play out over time on the optimization project.

I committed to the client that we, as a team, were going to fix the problems. And that we all shared responsibilities for the mess that we were in. Their management team did not buy into the concept initially, but as you will see, they came around.

We held a number of internal meetings with our leadership team and my services team where we discussed various options on how to resolve this broken relationship and broken software solution.

My services team and I developed a Lean Six Sigma approach, which we presented to our leadership team and which outlined how we were going to turn around this client into our best client with a superior regulatory solution.

We gained approval from our CEO and leadership team to move forward.

Our CEO attended the next meeting with the client where we laid out our plan.

I presented our Lean Six Sigma approach for the optimization project, which was well received but of course with some skepticism.

We used Six Sigma DMAIC (Define, Measure, Analyze, Improve, Control) as our framework to drive process excellence and manage the optimization project.

The relationship I developed with their project leader and the relationship our teams developed was critical to the success of the optimization project. Our joint teams quickly moved through forming, storming, norming and got to performing must faster that we all expected. We were bonded and on a mission.

The regulatory documents in question, material safety data sheet (MSDS) or safety data sheet (SDS), are very complex documents used around the world that contained, at the time, 16 sections (pages) of information and data.

The documents were produced in 37 languages and 13 different formats.

We developed a project charter and project plan with a small steering committee established to oversee the project.

The teams started our forensic work (Archaeologist) by completing a distribution and Pareto analysis of where the customizations were concentrated, which can be found on page 101.

Pareto Analysis is a statistical technique in decision-making used for the selection of a limited number of instances that will produce significant overall effect. It uses the Pareto Principle, also known as the 80/20 rule. The principle is that 20% of the instances will result in 80% of impact.[21]

The teams identified that four sections of the MSDS accounted for 58% of the customizations.

One section by itself accounted for 24% of the customizations.

No one had ever looked at the distribution of customizations before.

Using the Six Sigma approach, and the 5 Whys, the teams dug into the root cause analysis of the customizations.

Distribution and Pareto Analysis of Customizations

Chart of MSDS Customization Page Distribution

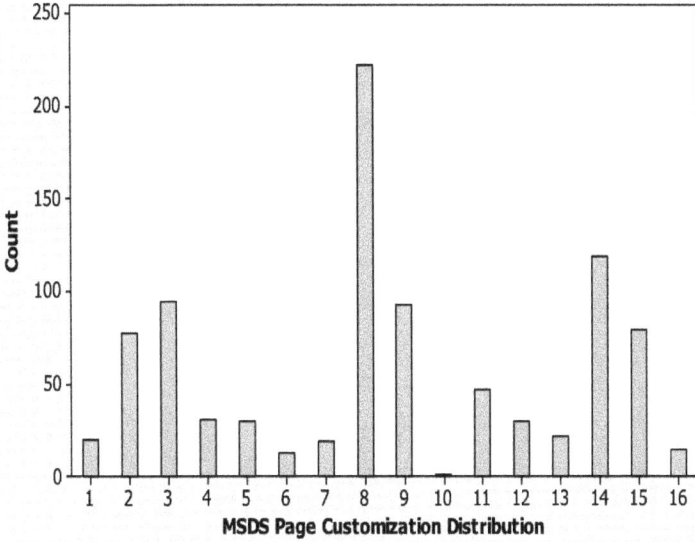

Pareto Chart of Page Customization Distribution

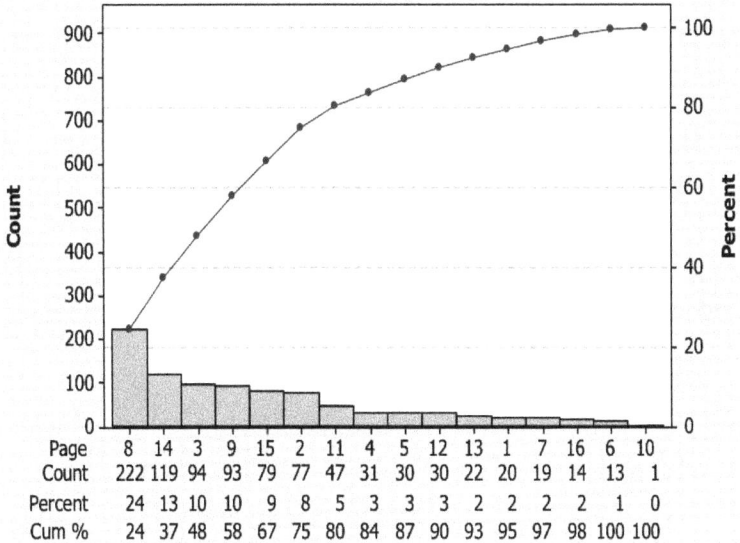

Page	8	14	3	9	15	2	11	4	5	12	13	1	7	16	6	10
Count	222	119	94	93	79	77	47	31	30	30	22	20	19	14	13	1
Percent	24	13	10	10	9	8	5	3	3	3	2	2	2	2	1	0
Cum %	24	37	48	58	67	75	80	84	87	90	93	95	97	98	100	100

Low and behold, we found an older gentleman in one of the offices who did not like the way some of the words came out of the regulatory software.

He thought it was not proper English!

And he was right!

It was proper regulatory terminology for the regulations, not proper English!

But 222 of the customizations centered around proper English!

Do you have any idea how much it cost first to implement and then maintain these customizations? A lot!

The team then interviewed the higher-level regulatory specialist who actually operated the solution and produced the documents.

The specialist did not like the proper English on the documents because they thought it was not proper regulatory terminology!

They thought the software was an unreliable and inaccurate regulatory solution because of this issue.

Here is the humor and irony of the situation ... and all of the convoluted steps that were taken resulting in a colossal mix-up!

Although the software generated the correct regulatory terminology, the customizations, when applied during the creation of the documents, would change it to proper English.

Then the regulatory specialist, who did not like the proper English, would edit the documents and change them back to the original regulatory terminology the system had generated in the first place.

The regulatory specialists did not know that the customizations had changed the documents.

Crazy what happens in business!

This is just one story about the customizations. There were many more, but none are as humorous as this one.

Case Conclusion

No one had looked at this level of detail and the end-to-end processes! There was no control over the system or processes that were producing one million+ regulatory documents on a global basis!

We found a number of additional process and technology issues during the analysis, including a number of hidden factories.

A hidden factory is an activity or set of activities in the process that result in reduction of quality or efficiency of a business process. Hidden factories are not known to others seeking to improve the process. Hidden factories are usually uncovered during current state analysis and documentation process. Six Sigma focuses on identifying and eliminating "hidden factory" activities.

The Five Stages of Grief

When we started to uncover what was going on with the customizations, there was little denial within the project teams.

But there was significant denial with the leadership teams.

When I presented the early findings to our leadership team, the person who had previously overseen the relationship with the client tried the blame the client.

When my counterpart presented the early findings to the client leadership team, they of course tried to blame us.

During our next joint meeting, tempers began to flare.

In particular, the client was angry at our company because they said we should have known better. It was our responsibility to maintain the integrity of our solution.

Our CEO, who had called into the meeting, explained that the person who had previously owned the solution on the client side told us to do what he said and not to challenge his decisions.

By the end of the meeting, cooler heads prevailed as we agreed on what we as cooperating partners all faced.

There was some negotiating as to the scope and timeline for the optimization project, but everyone knew we faced a lot of work ahead.

When we presented the expected results in headcount reduction, there was an overwhelming sadness with the client leadership team. Within this organization, the regulatory team had a clan culture.

The Clan Culture: This culture is rooted in collaboration. Members share commonalities and see themselves are part of one big family who are active and involved. Leadership takes the form of mentorship, and the organization is bound by commitments and traditions. The main values are rooted in teamwork, communication and consensus.

The regulatory team had worked together for many years and the leadership team knew that there were significant changes coming to their clan.

We were all directed to be very careful not to talk about what was going to happen as the leadership team worked their way through depression and finally to acceptance on the impact to their regulatory organization.

Corrective Action

1. Implemented a review process for any system modification. Required sign off from both the solution provider and the client.

2. Implemented a system-generated regulatory document "first" business process. Meaning the regulatory document generated by the software would be viewed as the standard regulatory document.

3. Implemented a review process for any alterations to system-generated regulatory documents. These required sign-offs by a manager and director before any alteration could be applied.

4. Implemented a Wave 1 de-customization project with plans for Wave 2 and 3 de-customization.

5. A significant reorganization took place around the globe.

6. Changed the process from manual to automated.

7. Established KPIs to manage continuous improvement during the improve and control stages.

8. Established a customer satisfaction survey distributed twice a year as part of the control, KPI system.

9. Eliminated the hidden factories.

Results

The Optimization project reduced customizations by greater than 80% in Wave 1 of de-customization.

By eliminating the customization, we were able to optimize the processes for creating the MSDS from manual, labor-intensive processes to an automated, system-generated MSDS.

In today's technology vernacular, we implemented a Robotic Process Automation (RPA) solution. This was pretty cutting edge for the time.

Through the automation, we reduced the regulatory staff headcount by 50%, from 80 regulatory specialists to 40 regulatory specialists in the first year of automation. Further reductions to the regulatory specialist staff were to come in subsequent years.

The optimization project saved the client multiple millions of dollars.

The client implemented a rigorous performance management system with KPIs to control ongoing performance and customer satisfaction.

Positive benefits came to their internal customers as customer satisfaction with this shared services organization increased tremendously.

The optimization project was phase one of a larger optimization and transformation program. Phase 2, transformation, was to be a complete digital transformation integrating a number of external systems to entirely automate the process of creating and maintaining MSDS.

A MEGA MYSTERY

This is, by far, my favorite transformation project story.

The business practice we will transform, Trade Promotion Management (TPM) has multi-levels of processes and an extensive cross-functional reach across the organization.

It was early one year when I received a call from my boss.

A project with a very strategic new client had been awarded to our firm.

My boss had little information about the exact nature of the project other than that I had been recommended by a number of people in our organization to lead the process transformation part of this project.

He asked me to give the VP who was overseeing the project a call to get the details.

I had never worked with the VP but knew him casually from multiple company meetings.

As he was explaining the project, Trade Promotion Management was a business practice area I had never heard of but knew peripherally.

For context, think promotions in a retail store like a buy one get one free (BOGO), which means the customer gets 50% off on the second item, usually for a limited time.

My role on the project would be as the process subject matter expert (SME).

We would have a project manager to manage the project and handle client relationships along with SMEs in technology, change management and consumer products. The firm also gave us good support staff through the appointment of junior consultants.

The client assembled an excellent project team.

Week Zero (0)

Week Zero (0) is usually a meet and greet week where the internal project team and the client project team start the Forming stage of team development. Forming with your internal team can be an enlightening experience or a total disaster. In this case, it was a great start to our relationship.

During Week Zero, you are reviewing the project charter getting alignment with the project goals and deliverables and maybe making a few tweaks for clarity. (Unfortunately, sometimes a major rewrite is required).

The project teams also review the project plan, and project timeline and again further align with the project goals and deliverables.

During this time, as part of the Forming Stage with the client Project Team, you are starting to understand the challenges the client is facing in particular business practices and interrelated processes.

Typically, at this stage, you are dealing with a tremendous number of "symptoms" and a fair share of bitching and moaning about anything that may be bugging the team members right now.

It is critical to use your best "listening and observation skills" as you are starting to pick up on the interactions between the client project team members (remember they are Forming) and how it relates to their organization's culture and cultural norms.

Here you are acting as the Anthropologist and Psychologist.

You're observing how people operate within their culture and the various personalities you'll be working with on the project.

Hopefully, you don't have to be the Psychiatrist this early in the project, but stranger things have happened!

You can see some real fireworks at this point as competing agendas amongst client project team members start to surface.

If you are fortunate to have a project team of "A" players with strong opinions and agendas, just sit back at this point and observe the dynamics. Take good notes about what you are hearing and seeing.

Who will come out victorious as client project team members strive for dominance?

You can also expect to see some of the first three stages of the five stages of grief: denial, anger and negotiating. Again, keep your listening and observation skills on high alert!!!

I am not saying this happened on this project. It is just a point of reference. I have experienced this on a number of other projects.

One of the interesting things about consulting is that your project teams come together from a virtual list of players from across the firm.

In many cases, you will have never seen, met, or heard of the people who have assembled for the project.

In this case, it was only the VP who I had never seen, met, or heard of.

Our project manager was a sharp, mid-career consultant from one of our practices. He had been selected with strong recommendations and a strong reputation.

We had two domain SMEs from our consumer products practice on the project.

After talking with them, I felt very comfortable and confident that I had a couple of "go-to" resources.

Our organizational change management SME was well respected within our firm.

Our main information technology resource, who was very well-versed in the TPM information technology used by the client, stayed with the project the entire time.

At different stages of the project, we added additional SMEs who brought specific skill sets to the project.

Later, we added another technology SME to the team.

The two junior consultants, one an early-career woman and the other an early-career man, both came with good recommendations from previous engagements.

We had an initial core team of eight, with additional resources coming and going during the project.

We had assembled a team of our own A-Players for the project. This was a very good situation.

The client project manager was the actual owner of the Trade Promotion Management at the company. He had owned the TPM processes for a number of years and was intimately involved with its evolution. I would quickly come to appreciate what a great guy he was.

A few of his team members were on the project; one was a manager, and one was a supervisor with two admins. The other seven members of the client team were "rising stars" of the organization.

This is what you want on your project team: A-Players!!!!!

From here, we'll follow the outline of business process transformation steps within this particular project.

Executive Sponsor and Steering Committee

During week zero, the project teams worked on a presentation that was to be given to the executive sponsor and steering committee at a team dinner on Wednesday night.

As I mentioned, this was a very high profile and strategic project for the client and our organization. Little did I know how strategic it would be until we reviewed the charter and developed the presentation for the dinner.

We had the opportunity to meet the executive sponsor, steering committee and additional executives at the dinner in a less formal atmosphere.

We actually started forming some relationships where if we met people in the hallways, we would be greeted with a warm smile and hello.

This organization had a great culture.

This company REALLY GOT IT!

The executive sponsor for the project was the EVP and COO, the #2 executive in the organization behind the chairman, president and CEO.

The steering committee was made up of a group of senior vice presidents and vice presidents.

This was a pretty exclusive group of executives, to say the least.

The dinner was very enjoyable.

The client project manager was on point with the presentation with a lot of good questions from the COO, steering committee and other attendees.

The project manager was also a Six Sigma Black Belt, so we got along very well.

During the development of the presentation, I asked him if there were many hidden factories in the TPM process.

Yes, Yes, Yes! There were hidden factories all over the place.

The client project manager put together a great, humorous slide about the hidden factories.

He showed a picture of an iceberg on the slide. In the part of the iceberg that is submerged, he had labeled it hidden factories. That was an awesome visual!

He explained to the audience the Six Sigma concept of hidden factories.

This brought a lot of chuckles and head-nodding, but then the COO interrupted and addressed the meeting.

"Ladies and gentlemen, this is our task at hand. Let's get rid of these hidden factories and operate trade promotion management as best in class!"

I love leaders that lead. Leaders that use clear, concise communication to get the team motivated and moving forward!

The only issue here, which we'll run into later on, is that the steering committee was all sales and marketing focused with the exception of the chief information officer(CIO).

There was no representation from supply chain or operations/manufacturing.

Who from the leadership team is not on the steering committee?

I always like to know the answer to this question.

We would find the steering committee to be very diligent and disciplined about their responsibilities for this strategic transformation project.

As we progressed through the early weeks of the project, our change management SME did an excellent job interviewing and dialoguing with the members of the steering committee.

Doing this was extremely important to the project as "executive alignment" is critical in making sure everyone is on the "same page" as the project begins.

The monthly steering committee meeting works toward keeping the alignment and making decisions.

Many times, on a project, I have been the change management SME.

One of the first things I do is develop a questionnaire with the client project manager for my interviews with the steering committee and/or executive team.

I coordinate my interviews with the head of HR when possible, and in a number of cases, they sit in on the interviews.

I ask the steering committee and/or executive team individually the same set of questions to determine if there are any "gaps" in alignment.

You'll usually find leaders may have different objectives relative to their particular areas of responsibility, i.e., sales, marketing and supply chain.

Organization

This company is a great American company. I mean a *great American* Company.

In my opinion, this organization has a clan culture.

Even though this company has a clan culture, it does not mean that it does not show elements of adhocracy, market and hierarchy cultures. There are elements, but the dominant culture is a clan culture.

The members of the organization have known each other for many, many years. They have built friendships over those long periods.

They are a family who can be brutally honest with each other in meetings and then go out and laugh at themselves and each other. I noted very self-deprecating humor when I was there.

As consultants, we are usually, if not always on the outside looking in. We are charged with observing the camaraderie or dysfunction of organizations.

As we worked on this project over the initial few weeks, we were able to see and appreciate the unique culture this organization lived by each day.

If they liked you, you were a member of the family.

I'm not exactly sure who coined my nickname or when it was coined, but I became: The Dragonman.

I'd go into the steering committee meeting, and one executive, in particular, would comment: "The Dragonman is here. We must be doing something wrong!"

I would sit next to him and have a few laughs as I gave him my version of CliffsNotes for the project.

This organization had a "get things done" attitude. They believed nothing was impossible if they worked together as a team.

The project manager would share that they were known to "knock down walls" to get their aim accomplished.

As we worked through the project, he came to realize that they would knock down walls but with sometimes significant collateral damage.

The project manager came to appreciate that our team was showing their organization new ways not to take a frontage assault but to remove a brick or two from the wall and help it fall down more gracefully and with less fallout. When that happened, the entire team could charge forward and reap the rewards.

We want to minimize collateral damage!

One real problem we ran into was with the supply chain and manufacturing/operations leadership.

As I mentioned, they were not part of the steering committee.

The project obviously had high visibility across the organization, and they had not been included on the steering committee.

The supply chain and manufacturing/operations team were standoffish.

The TPM processes we were going to transform predominately related to sales and marketing processes; but they did have a significant and direct influence on the supply chain and manufacturing/operations.

It took some backroom intervention to get the supply chain and manufacturing/operations teams to cooperate.

I'm not sure how far up the organization it had to go before the cooperation clicked into place.

And there were some negative feelings that never really went away.

I use the word "cooperate" rather than "engage" as it was more cooperation than engagement in this case.

Business Process

Trade Promotion Management is complex.

The management of TPM happens through a number of detailed processes and software applications that assist companies in managing the complexity of TPM activities.

As I mentioned earlier, I kind of knew what TPM was, but I did not know the processes that were going on behind the scenes.

Here are the processes that we used (and you can follow along with the Trade Promotion Management Processes chart below):

- The level 0 process is trade promotion management.
- There are three level 1 processes: planning, execution and advanced selling.
- Under the planning process, there are nine level 2 processes.
- Under the execution process, there are six level 2 processes.
- Under the advanced selling process, there are six level 2 processes.
- Under each level 2 process, there are multiple level 3 processes.

TPM Business Processes

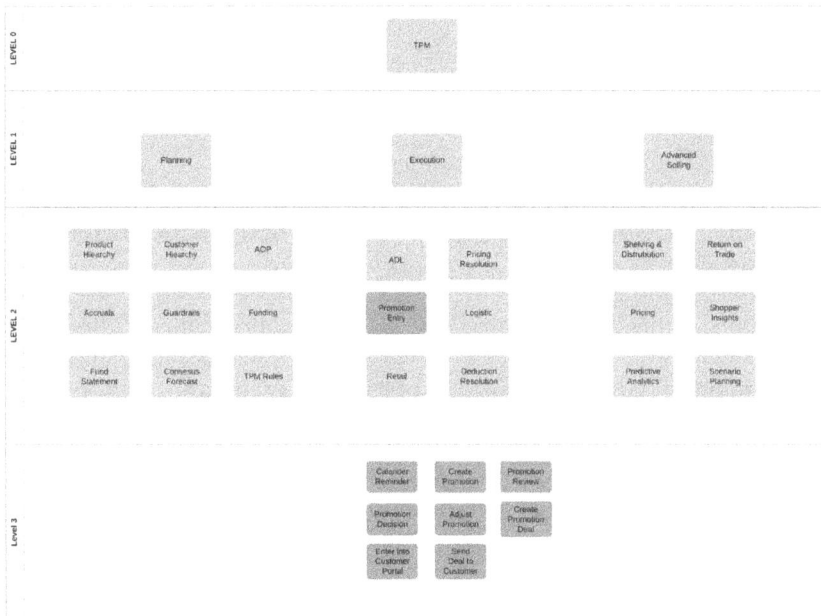

Wow, that was a pretty simple transformation!

Not!

And don't forget, I really am not an expert in this area!

Yikes!

I would come to learn that trade promotion management is one of the most administratively complicated and tedious "clusters" of intertwined processes I have ever seen.

The management and administration of the TPM processes can be mind-numbing.

So, where do we start?

The existing TPM processes had been put into place a number of years previous when the client had implemented their TPM technology solution.

The processes had evolved and morphed since this implementation.

Of course, none of the TPM processes had been documented, so this would be the beginning of our journey, documenting the current state or "as-is" processes.

The client project manager was a Six Sigma Black Belt as I mentioned, so we decided to use process flow maps with swim lanes to document the processes down to level 3 across the 21 level 2 processes.

When appropriate, using cross-functional business process flows, also known as swim lane diagram, is the best way I have seen to document complex processes.

I have gotten away from value stream maps as it takes too long to educate everyone on all the symbols.

Straight-forward process flow maps get the job done for me, and they are easy to understand.

If you prefer value stream maps, go for it.

The plan was that the client project manager was going to lead the documentation efforts, and we would monitor and provide guidance.

We would bring in members of the client project team to be part of the documentation process when their area of expertise was required.

Our entire project team, business and technical, sat in on all of the process documentation workshops.

Before we get into the details of the work, let's discuss a Six Sigma methodology that we'll use for root cause analysis, the 5 Whys.

The 5 Whys is an iterative interrogative technique used to explore the cause-and-effect relationships underlying a particular problem. "The primary goal of the technique is to determine the root cause of a defect or problem by repeating the question 'Why?' Each answer forms the basis of the next question. The "5" in the name derives from an anecdotal observation on the number of iterations needed to resolve the problem. Not all problems have a single root cause."[22]

If you wish to uncover multiple root causes, the method must be repeated while asking a different sequence of questions each time.

It is helpful to have some knowledge of the process, comparing to leading practices seen in the industry.

But not knowing the process keeps you away from "preconceived notions."

You keep the questioning going as long as it takes to gain consensus on the root cause or root causes.

The 5 Whys method is only as good as the knowledge, honesty and persistence of the people involved.

Hopefully, you can get to the root cause(s) before the 5 Whys, and heaven help us if we have to go to 6 or 7 Whys.

You may need to be the Psychiatrist at this point!

Here are some thoughts on how to approach the 5 Whys:

1. It is necessary to engage the process owner and some process participants in the 5 Whys process. The process owner and participants have knowledge of the existing processes. Having domain subject matter experts (SMEs) can be helpful as they understand the process outside the client context.

2. Use a whiteboard, flip-chart, or a computer so that everyone can see the 5 Whys.

3. Write down the problem and make sure that everyone involved understands it.

4. As you start to hear symptoms, work to identify the causes.

5. You should start to pick up on some of the cause-and-effect relationships.

6. Make sure that root cause(s) leads to the problem you are discussing. If you start to get sidetracked, put it on a parking lot list for later review.

7. Work toward clarity and consensus and getting everyone on the same page.

8. Stay disciplined.

9. Focus on the facts and the process.

10. Don't make it personal. A person is never the root cause. Unless it's the CEO! ;-)

11. Be open and honest but maintain decorum.

12. Try to get to the root cause before the 5th Why but don't be surprised if you reach 6 or 7 Whys.

13. The Root Cause must be agreed to by all participants. You must have a unanimous jury!

Here's an example of a 5 Whys Worksheet:

The Five Whys

DEFINE THE PROBLEM

↓

Why is this happening?

↓

Why is that?

↓

Why is that?

↓

Why is that?

↓

Why is that?

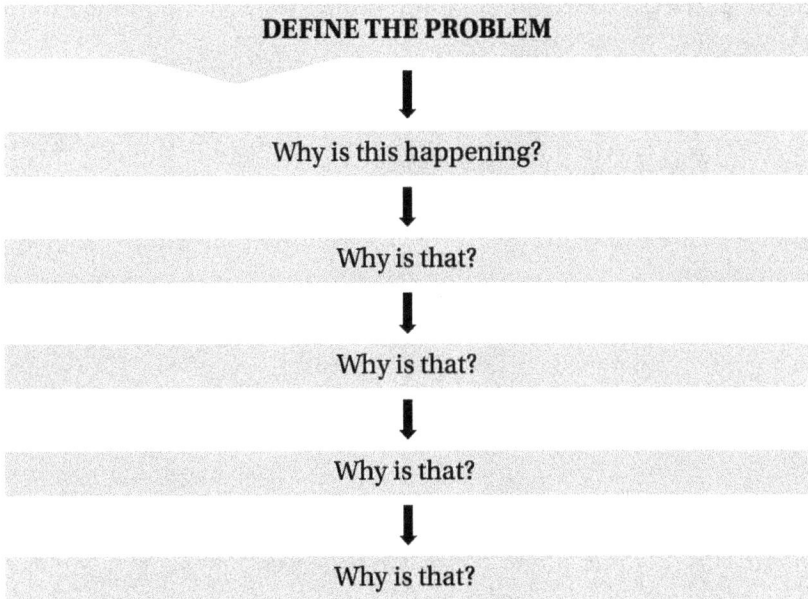

When you go through the 5 Whys process, most if not all of the answers to Why #1 will be symptoms.

At Why #2, the predominance will still be symptoms, but you may start getting a feel for the root cause(s).

You need to work your way through the 5 Whys until you feel that the root cause(s) has been identified and clarified and you are able to reach a consensus agreement.

Most likely, there will still need to be some clarification around the root cause, but by Why 5 you should you have it identified.

Plan to see the teams in a state of euphoria and enlightenment. The lights have been turned on.

Or ... there may be total PANIC!!!!!! And people positively hitting the 5 Stage of Grief!

I love this part of the transformation processes because this is where "I solve mysteries!!!!"

The concept of the 5 Whys is relatively straightforward, but I will offer some insights and a word of caution.

When you are going through the 5 Whys analysis, meetings can get volatile and sometimes personal. Of course, you want to steer away from personal attacks.

And ... during the 5 Whys process, you will wear many hats as we talked about earlier.

- **The Archaeologist** because your artifacts will be the process maps, symptoms and knowledge.

- **The Anthropologist** as you identify what cultural elements are at issue with the root cause(s).

- **The Detective** asking the questions to uncover the clues. In my opinion, the 5 Whys could be called the 5 Questions because each Why is actually a clarification question.

- **The Conductor, the maestro,** as you are directing the 5 Whys performance. You are wearing all the hats. During the 5 Whys performance, you bring the ensemble members together to solve the mysteries.

- **The Psychologist,** because many raw emotions will come from process mapping and the 5 Whys conversation. As the Conductor and Psychologist, you have to manage the volatility and inter-action of team members. These conversations can get pretty pointed and at times, abusive.

- **The Psychiatrist** because you can or will see abnormal human behavior. During this process, who the loose cannons are on the team become more than evident. Beware, these people could be on your team!

This is where I get a rush. I love to solve mysteries and wear all these hats in the process!

When you get into the meetings with the teams and start the 5 Whys and decomposition of the process(s), it is a highly emotionally charged environment.

Tempers flare. Anger explodes. Fingers get pointed, and blame is assigned as the performance starts to unfold in front of you.

As the Conductor, it is paramount that you "direct the performance" of the teams and control the environment.

You do have to let things play out to see what is uncovered and where the conversation goes, but you do have to "direct the performance" of the teams and control the environment as well.

You have to be a keen observer of who is performing (talking) and who is not performing (staying silent).

As the conversations crescendo, are the silent participants buying into the train of thought, or are they naysayers who are just checking out?

You have to observe everyone in the room and make a determination as to where they are in the performance.

You have to direct questions to those who are staying silent to gather their input.

Like a maestro, you are bringing in different instruments to highlight a particular part of the performance.

In many performances, I have seen a dominant personality trying to control the direction of the conversation.

This is likely because it is their area being flushed out. You can imagine they will get defensive.

You cannot let this happen as you must keep control of the performance!

This is where you may see a "sleight of hand," or you may note the "Teflon manager" trying to direct the conversation away from the root cause to blame others.

You cannot let this happens.

Will you piss off some people by keeping the conversations on track?

Yes, this is your job.

This is where you get under people's skins. Still, you cannot let things get out of control.

This work is not for the "faint of heart"!

Let's transition here a bit to discuss concepts around institutional and tribal knowledge and hidden factories.

Because the knowledge you are gaining through the 5 Whys is institutional and tribal knowledge!

Institutional knowledge comprises the understanding of processes, systems, details, standards, folklore, cultural values and general information that make up an organization.

Institutional knowledge or institutional memory is the stored collective knowledge or memory of the organization.[23]

It has been defined or collected over the lifespan of the organization.

It is not documented knowledge; it is known knowledge.

Tribal knowledge is any unwritten information that is not commonly known by others within an organization.

It is known to tribe members, i.e., departments and/or specific job functions.

Tribal knowledge is siloed.[24]

This term is used most when referencing information that may need to be known by others to perform a process, produce a product, or deliver a service.

Tribal knowledge is a term often associated with a Six Sigma.

It is often referred to as knowledge "known" yet undocumented.

It is information that has been handed down from generation to generation or worker to worker with no known documentation.

It is knowledge contained within a group that is assumed to be factual but has no known proof to verify that it is factual.

Institutional and tribal knowledge is typically not documented. The knowledge is in the minds of individuals.

Institutional and tribal knowledge is where you find that "it's the way we do it or the way we've always done things."

Note: Institutional knowledge and tribal knowledge will provide a lot of symptoms and policies. A symptom can also be a policy.

A policy, either written or unwritten, is a principle to guide decisions through logical or controlled outcomes.

A policy is a statement of intent.

Some are written, but many are not.

When we document the symptoms and/or policies, we are now creating "artifacts" that can be used in your role as the Archaeologist.

The symptoms and policies are artifacts, but they can also provide a view of the cultural.

This is where we are in our role as the Anthropologist.

What is the culture for decision making?

Understanding the culture for decision making relates to what we have uncovered in the root cause analysis.

Hidden Factories

What you also find during this process are the hidden factories.

The hidden factory is an activity or set of activities in the process that result in the reduction of quality or efficiency of a business process.

They are not known to others seeking to improve the process. Six Sigma focuses on identifying and eliminating "hidden factory" activities.

As you map the current state processes, the hidden factories appear.

The client project team will start to add a new swim lane (swim lanes are used to establish a process participant)for a process participant and/or new process steps through the iterations.

This is typically where the hidden factories are identified. It's these people or process steps that may not be visible even to the leader of the process area.

Using the 5 Whys methodology, we will identify symptoms, institutional and tribal knowledge and hidden factories.

Time to put everything into practice.

As you can imagine, the first few workshops were exceptionally challenging as we started to document the current state or as-is process.

We did a rough cut of the TPM processes by establishing the swim lanes and taking a macro look at the major process steps. That was tough enough to get consensus.

Then we put in the more detailed processes steps and started to connect the flow between the process steps as we worked our way down the levels.

What we got was a tangled conglomeration of TPM process steps and process flows.

During this exercise, someone on the team would regularly say that we missed a process step or process flow.

In many cases, these were the hidden factories. So we added them to the process flows.

This was obviously an iterative process as this was the first time, the client project team had ever seen all the processes documented from level 0 to level 3.

See the following page for a look at the current state of the level 3 process for promotion entry.

During the documentation process, the five stages of grief appeared in the emotions of the client project team.

Denial that things were not as bad as they looked.

Anger as to how they could have let these processes get so convoluted.

Negotiating to fix what was wrong relatively quickly.

Depression in that the problem was worse than they realized and would be a lot of work to make right.

Acceptance that the work must be done to improve.

This is not usual!!!

This is reality!!!

This is what I see on every optimization or transformation project!!

Promotion Entry Current State

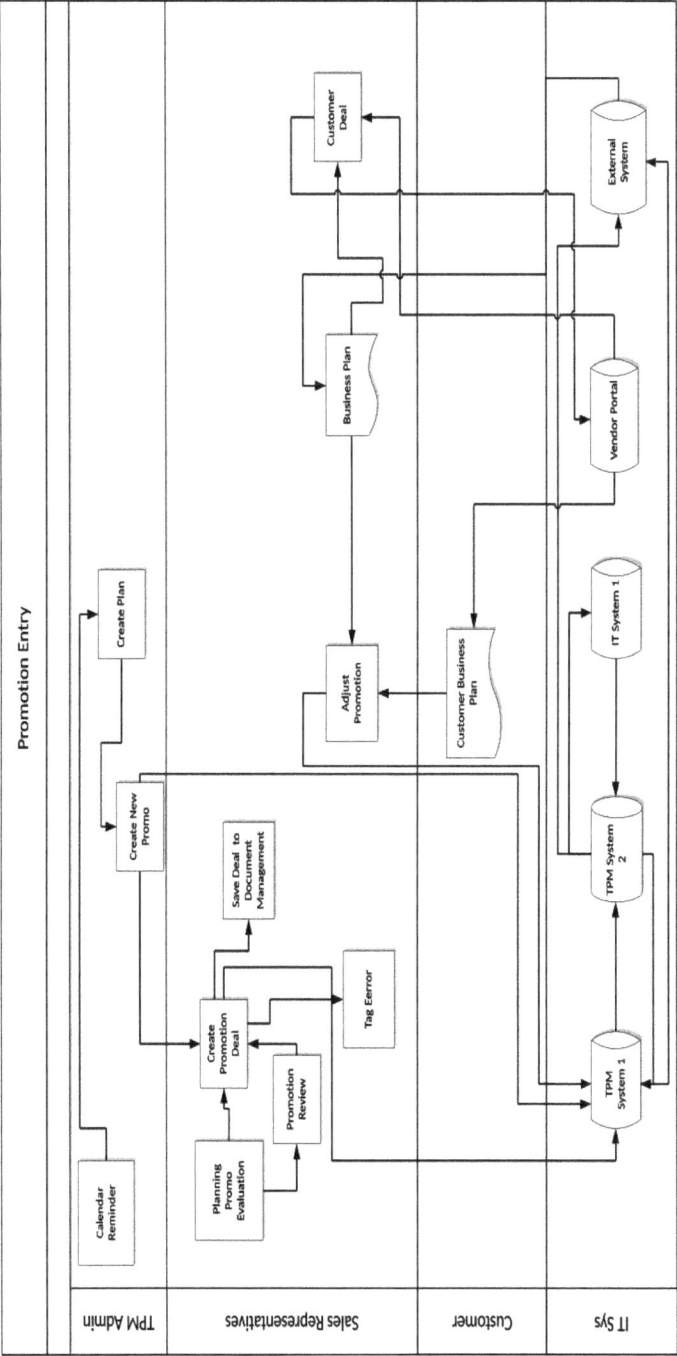

Promotion Entry

Swimlanes (bottom labels): TPM Admin | Sales Representatives | Customer | IT Sys

TPM Admin: Calendar Reminder; Create New Promo; Create Plan

Sales Representatives: Planning Promo Evaluation; Create Promotion Deal; Promotion Review; Save Deal to Document Management; Tag Error; Adjust Promotion; Business Plan; Customer Deal

Customer: Customer Business Plan

IT Sys: TPM System 1; TPM System 2; IT System 1; Vendor Portal; External System

The client really doesn't know all their processes at a granular level.

They just go about their everyday jobs and perform all of the processes.

After we had the processes documented and received consensus from the client project team, we started the detective work looking for clues.

The teams were now moving rapidly into performing!

With a consensus on the TPM process maps, we moved to the exciting part of using the 5 Whys and identifying the root cause(s).

With the full client project team in place, we started walking through each of the level 2 processes and level 3 process.

We color-coded the level 3 processes as red for an extremely broken process and yellow for a moderately broken process.

During this analytical process, we used the 5 Whys to probe deeper into "Why" using red or yellow to get past the symptoms and to the root cause of the problem with the process step.

Green represents a non-broken process.

We thought we had all the hidden factories called out but au contraire!

The client project manager was surprised when we started adding additional hidden factories.

The client project team had a few members from the project manager's team on the project in the form of one manager and one supervisor with two admins.

As we were documenting the processes, it was these team members who had identified the initial hidden factories, and now we were adding more subtle hidden factories.

These were the team members who were in the trenches and doing the work on a daily basis.

They were in many cases the actual hidden factory!

It was at this particular stage that the process maps got really messy with completely visible hidden factories.

The client project manager had not realized the total depth of work his team was doing in the hidden factories.

At one point when we added a new hidden factory, he asked the manager, "Is this another hidden factory?"

"Yes, because the processes are so broken, this is the work we have to do to get things done!"

It took only a few of these exchanges before the client project manager stopped asking the question.

The client had built an industrial complex with factories hidden all over the place.

What is described here is typical and a serious disconnect between management and day-to-day operations.

When organizations don't have their processes documented, subsequently there is no visibility of the actual work being done.

To correct these situations, the question is, does the organization have the ability to culturally come together to objectively face the work required to document the processes in a non-blaming, collaborative manner?

This can be a true game-changer for the betterment of all!

In this project, we had "the A-Team" on the project with a number of assertive personalities.

We had a lot of robust conversations during our working sessions.

The unique thing about this company's culture was that they could fight like cats and dogs during the session, and at the end, breathe a big sigh of relief at a job well done.

Then it was time to go get a few drinks if it was the end of our afternoon session.

On more than one occasion the next morning, one of the rising stars would complement the team on what a good session we had the previous day.

We were getting past symptoms to root cause(s) and exposing the real issues.

They would usually preface the conversation by saying what a "tough crowd" it was and that they had a unique culture.

Tough crowd, huh? I have seen worse.

Unique culture? Positively! They had a freaking awesome culture!

We appreciated the comments on a job well done.

When you combine the use of the color-coded current state process analysis and the 5 Whys, you can really focus on those areas which have the biggest issues or constraints in the processes, and you can start working on your root cause analysis.

On the following page is an example of the color-coded level 3 promotion entry process.

I like to begin the review from top to bottom and left to right color coding in the subprocess boxes. We are identifying where the broken subprocesses are by using red and yellow, which for our purposes in this book, are identified by gray and white. By default, any subprocess that is not red or yellow is green, identified by black here. For a better interpretation of this chart, please refer to the legend supplied that indicates which gradient applies to red, yellow, or green.

I am not saying that the red or yellow subprocess is where the root cause resides. Because most likely, this is where the symptoms are felt from the root cause.

Using the 5 Whys and diving down to the lower level of symptoms, you will find that the root cause(s) is in many cases upstream from the current process and is affecting the downstream processes.

A cascading effect from an upstream process(s) occurs, which is where the actual root cause resides.

Knowing that you can have a cascading effect is very important when doing root cause analysis and determining cause and effect relationships.

The red process is the effect, and the cause is actually not even resident in the current process. It resides in the previous process(s). The cause lights up the downstream processes to be either red or yellow.

Promotion Entry Current State – Color-Coded

Promotion Entry

RED ■   GREEN □
YELLOW ▨   ▨

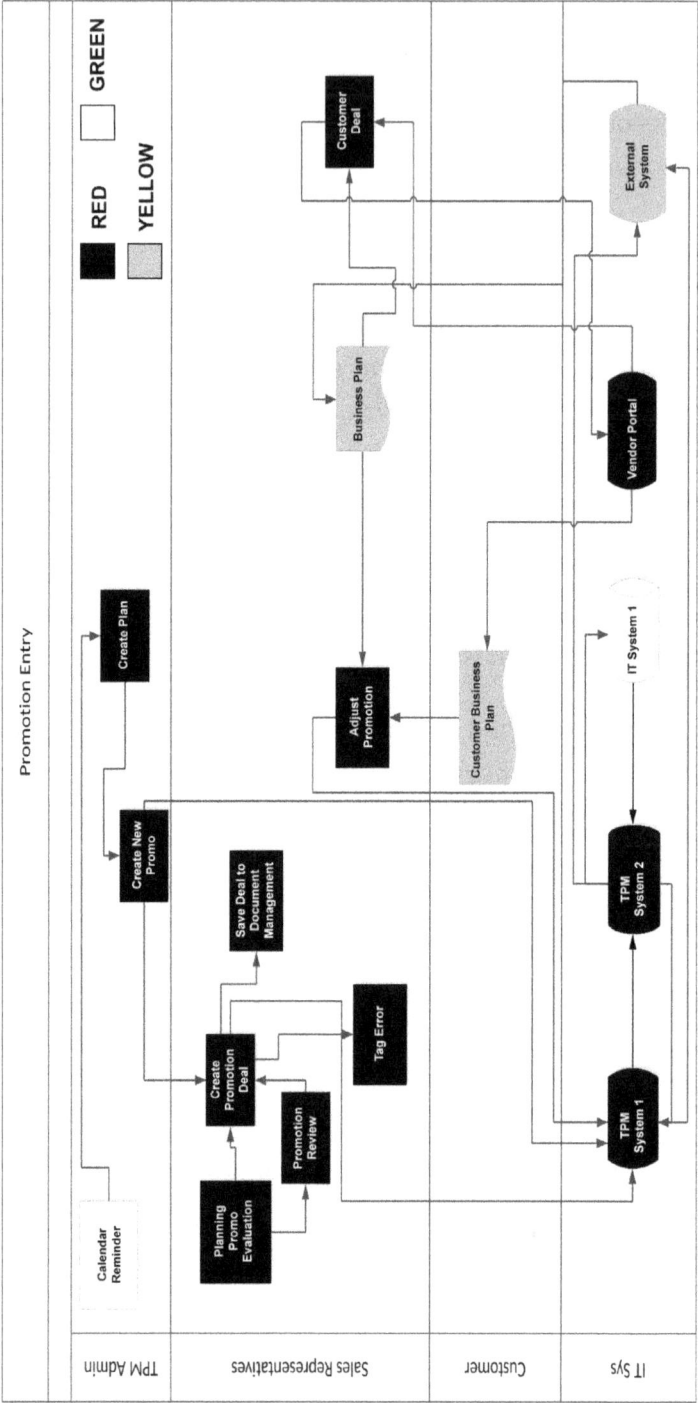

| TPM Admin | Sales Representatives | Customer | IT Sys |

The Problem with Silos

Silos are detrimental to any organization, but this is an old story that's been around for a long time.

I see it on every project, whether the company is 100 years old or 10 years old.

> **Silos are detrimental to any organization, but this is an old story that's been around for a long time. I see it on every project, whether the company is 100 years old or 10 years old.**

The silos form; communication breaks down, and problems manifest themselves because no one is looking at the big picture and the integration of the silos.

Many times, you hear that silos need to be torn down. I don't agree with that as it has a negative connotation that something is wrong with one or each silo.

We are really looking to integrate the silos.

In the Organization chapter, I relate silos to subcultures. Each department's subculture can have an effect on how it communicates and collaborates with other departments.

When organizations operate with well-constructed silos, knowledge and data is solely contained within the individual silo (department).

The knowledge and data would be beneficial to other departments to make their operations more effective and efficient, but owning silos bottles up that benefit.

At times working in and with silos seems like a cat and mouse game.

I was working in a paper mill which was experiencing operational issues.

A paper mill has a "wet end" where the slurry of paper fibers, fillers and additives is created and a "dry end" where the finished paper is produced.

The wet end and the dry end were well-constructed silos. They did not talk to each other.

If an issue arose in the wet end that could impact the dry end, the wet end never shared the information.

They would just throw the problem over the fence to the dry end.

Quality issues were abundant.

Silos were not talking to each other.

A classic example of business silos is sales & operations.

Sales & operations are like oil and water.

The subcultures of sales and operations are usually very different.

Even if you shake them up and emulsify them into a solution, they will quickly fall apart and revert to their original forms.

Silos, in many cases, are caused by conflicting goals.

Sales wants to sell anything and everything, Operations wants to produce what it knows it can efficiently and economically. Never the twain shall meet.

The impact on employees is great.

It's an "us vs. them" mentality that has embedded itself in the organization.

Another classic silo confrontation is IT vs. the rest of the company!!

Enough said on that one …

In Six Sigma Black Belt training, they emphasize that most quality problems happen when there are handoffs from one operation or department to the next.

Silos exacerbate the handoff problems when knowledge and data are not shared.

The symptom of the root cause may be felt in multiple silos, but because organizations don't look at the cause and effect of relationships across the silos, the root cause takes hold and affects many parts of the organization.

The root cause may be in one of the initial processes in one solo and have a negative effect on the subsequent downstream processes in different silos.

So, if you fix the root cause which fixes the initial process, then the downstream process is cleared and turned green.

Also, be on the lookout when changing a red or yellow process to green. Before you do that, ask yourself if it will turn other process(s) on the process map to red or yellow.

It's important to note; you have not really gotten to the root cause if this happens. Instead, you are fixing a symptom(s).

Additionally, be on the lookout where if you change the process(s) to green in the current process, it will have a cascading effect of turning the process(s) of an upstream or downstream process red or yellow.

This is another case where you are resolving symptoms, but where the true root cause resides in an entirely different process.

Now, this is where you have to be careful. You must validate what is truly the root cause through multiple process reviews and triangulation with other processes.

Note: Here is an interesting fact, and it is so very important: The true root cause may not even be on the radar screen when you start a project. This means that when the project starts, people have preconceived notions about what their problems are and what they will be trying to fix. However, experience has shown that in many cases, the client project team's assumptions are invalid. In actuality, they have no idea where the true problem/root cause lies.

One root cause our teams identified on the project was quite critical to the processes and had a cascading effect across every process.

This root cause was not really on the radar screen when we started the project, but it became a major focus.

It was crazy how one issue had such a profound effect on the *organization*, not only the processes.

The root cause was pricing.

Think about a company that produces products for retail.

They can produce hundreds if not thousands of products.

The synchronization and maintenance of pricing needed to run the company successfully are mind-boggling not only inside the company but also as it pertains to all of their customers.

Pricing touches so many parts of the organization: sales, marketing, finance, legal and IT.

Making changes to pricing policies and practices is a true cross-functional effort, and it takes time to unravel and readjust.

The client team gradually came to grips as to the ramifications to the organization.

The gravity of the situation took time to resonate, which it usually does with an issue of this magnitude — as well as multiple rounds of discussion were needed to plan how it was going to be resolved.

This is where you need a strong client project manager and a strong "A" project team.

The client project manager and project team members are the ones who translate the culture and language of the organization.

The client project manager and project team need to "own" the conversation and sell the resolution to the steering committee. Of course, with your help and support.

If you are running an internal transformation project, with hopefully an "A" team, your team has to be able to step up and articulate your findings to the steering committee.

Knowing that the steering committee may be skeptical of your findings, come prepared both with documentation (artifacts) and with the team onboard.

You'll need some intestinal fortitude to deliver the truth, maybe about some unpleasant news like pricing.

As we have discussed, this type of work is not for the faint of heart!

The Five Stages of Grief

Were our findings surprising to the steering committee?

Yes and no.

Yes, in the fact that the steering committee was surprised at the depth of the problem that pricing had across the company.

No, in the fact that there had been some concerns amongst a few members of the steering committee about pricing.

I was very impressed with the way the steering committee handled the meeting. We did not see what I see in many situations — denial and anger. They asked lot a great questions. And our project teams were well prepared to answer those questions.

Again, you have to remember, members of the steering committee may have had a significant hand in establishing what came to be the root cause that is identified.

They could have been the Architects of the root cause (in this case pricing) when they were in more junior positions or recently had implemented the root cause, pricing, when they were in their current jobs.

Remember these are sales and marketing leaders on the steering committee who deal with pricing all the time.

It took a while to get to acceptance by the steering committee based on the magnitude of the root cause.

Future State Design Process

The first part of the future state design is to incorporate the changes coming from addressing the root cause and pricing.

Pricing had an effect on so many of the level-3 processes.

The project teams worked together to refine the processes to build the future state design through a couple of iterations based on leading practices.

We were able to change red processes to yellow or green and yellow processes to green.

When we were done with the future state design, there were no more red processes, but a few yellow processes remained. Again, for the easiest translation of these colors to the gray gradient scale, please refer to the legends on the applicable diagrams.

The future state design eliminated most of the hidden factories. The ones that remained were not hidden anymore, and we had a better understanding of why they existed in the first place.

Future State Information Technology Design

The client had implemented a rather cutting-edge TPM solution to manage the TPM processes.

Our technology team developed the future state TPM solution based on current industry methodologies.

The technology team sat in on all of the future state process discussions so that we would be able to align with the future state TPM solution.

Not all the red processes were strictly related to the root cause.

A number of the red processes identified hidden factories related to workarounds of the TPM solution. There had been no continuous improvement done to the TPM solution and business processes for many years, only additions.

Our Industry SMEs were able to identify leading practices which allowed us to build more efficient and effective future state processes aligned with the future state TPM solution, eliminating additional hidden factories.

Future State Process and IT Solution

On the following page is the future state process map updated for the new promotion entry processes and a new TPM solution.

This is obviously a lot cleaner and more efficient than the current state promotion entry processes. You'll see that many of the process steps were removed as well as one of the TPM systems.

Organizational Change Management

As I mentioned in the section on executive sponsor and steering committees, this company got change management right for our project.

Promotion Entry Future State

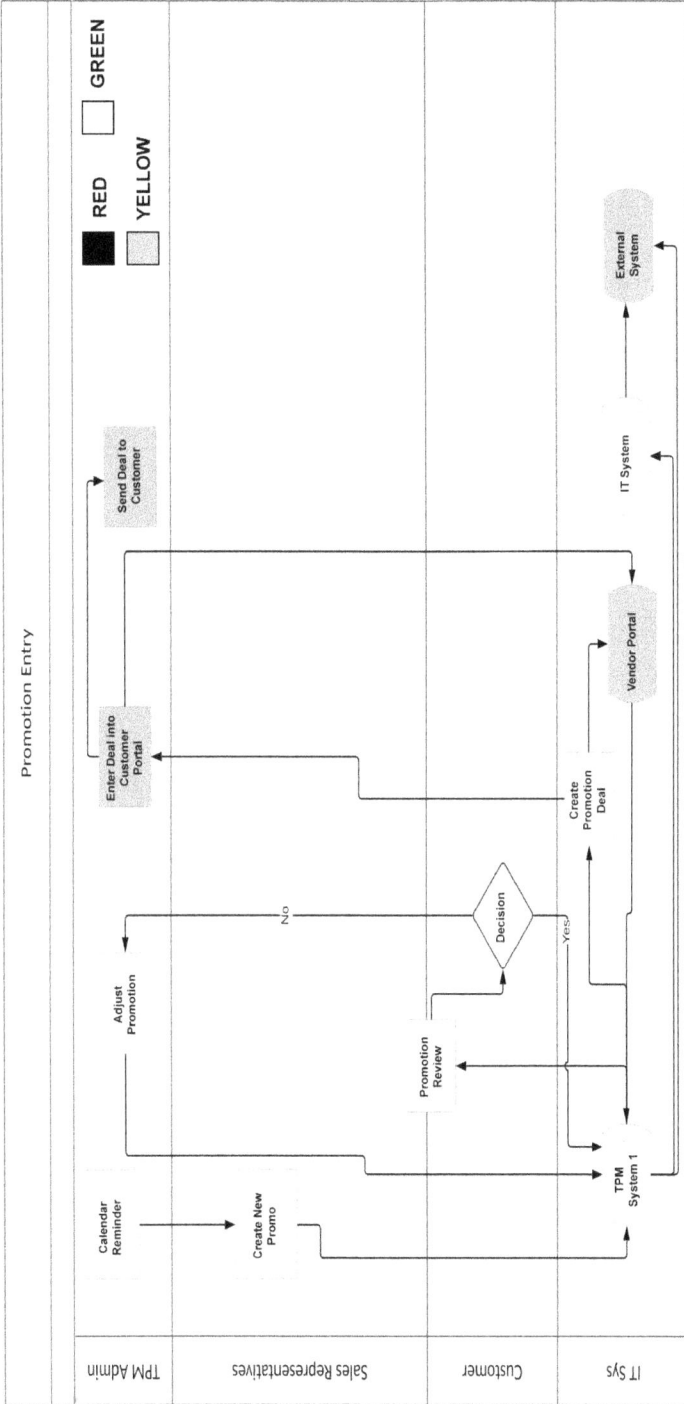

Our VP, during the sales cycle, informed the client that without an organizational change management workstream, we would pass on the project.

Congratulations to him as I have seen countless sales teams cave in on the organizational change management workstream.

And it comes back to bite the engagement team in the ass.

In many cases, the sales teams and client leaders don't get organization change management, as they believe organizational change management is "fluff."

I don't blame them, and I don't entirely disagree. I've seen less than robust change management programs.

This client selected an experienced leader from their organization to be the organizational change management leader for the workstream.

There were a lot of good reasons for this.

This gentleman had been with the company for many years and was well-respected across all aspects of the organization.

He was known as someone who got things done and had been placed in high profile roles on high profile projects in the past.

He knew of the dissatisfaction with the current TPM systems and processes very well.

He lived it every day with his teams and had been a strong proponent of the need to get better controls with a new vision and a sense of urgency.

He participated in many of the current state workshops and was a vocal observer that offered keen insights as we were working our ways through the process documentation and the 5 Whys.

The A-Players from the project really helped drive at sometimes challenging conversations.

They were done with the past many years, and it was now time to move forward.

This was their chance to put their imprint on the future.

As I mentioned, these were the rising-star leaders of the organization, and they wanted to get the future right.

As the Conductor of the sessions, it was my job to orchestrate and guide these conversations.

In a number of sessions, these rising leaders would get a bit frustrated with the perceived resistance to change.

At this point, as the Conductor, I had to step in to orchestrate the conversation.

It is critical that these conversations occur before you have to go to the steering committee.

You don't want to go to the steering committee to solve these kinds of conflicts. And I said that very thing to them.

"You were put on the project to solve problems, not perpetuate existing ones!"

Business Case for Change: What Are Our Future State Strategies?

Steering committees want to know what they are getting for their money and what the organization is up against when working to implement the recommendations.

When dealing with the future state, as the strategist, you need to develop a storyline and the business case for change.

In the storyline, you are presenting to the steering committee documentation concerning why the project team has come up with the specific recommendations and the impact on the project and organization.

We used a variety of documentation tools to educate the steering committee on the directions of our recommendations.

On the following page are a few examples of the documentations and overview of a number of recommendations we used.

Our aim is to identify what the category or focus area for the recommendation is.

We are qualifying the recommendations by the impact on the organization, effort to implement the recommendation, and how difficult the recommendation will be to implement from a change management standpoint.

These qualifications are subjective based on a collaborative discussion with the project teams.

Qualifications and Recommendations

Category	Recommendation	Impact	Effort	Change
Efficiency	Establish a...	High	High	High
Efficiency	Select a XYZ system to...	High	High	High
Efficiency	Expand the adoption of...	High	High	High
Efficiency	Change ABC policy to...	High	Medium	Low
Efficiency	Create a master...	High	High	Medium
Efficiency	Create a central repository for...	High	High	Medium
Efficiency	Reduce the complexity of our...	Medium	Low	Low
Efficiency	Allocate DEF to the regions...	Medium	Low	Medium
Efficiency	Develop an understanding of the root causes between...	Medium	High	Medium
IT	Develop electronic interfaces between...	Medium	High	Medium

Within the context of a Business Case for Change, on the following page is an example of a business benefits template that we used.

Business Benefits – Efficiency

Business Area

Interest Areas	1. Promotion Entry
	1. Reduce upfront administration and reduce number of clicks/entries
	2. Eliminates error
	3. Simplifies the matching process
	4. Improve forecast accuracy
	5. Align data
	2. Root Causes – Policy
	1. Reduce the impact of policy vs. policy conflicts
	2. Identify Pricing root cause issues that impact price discrepancy and update processes to fix issues
	3. Reduce deductions, price discrepancies
	4. Reduce fees
Examples	• Setup a promotion on all SKUs that are being promoted at the same time
	• Reduce the number of Promo Groups
	• Manipulating shipping dates to meet customer expectations
Financial Target	• Reduction of post audit payouts
	• Reallocation of staff to value added activities
	• Improve customer payments
KPIs / Metrics	• First Time Accuracy, Forecast Accuracy, % Pricing Discrepancies, DSO

In the next example, the template we used to capture the essence of our Recommendations, we discuss the impact on each of the functional areas.

The last part of the recommendation templates is where we clearly articulated language for our 60-second elevator pitch. The 60-second elevator pitch is a short, focused description of the recommendation.

The 60-second elevator pitch was worked on very closely with the project teams as it was critical to communicate and educate the direction of the recommendations.

We developed a 60-second elevator pitch for the overall project and for each recommendation.

Recommendation: Develop Electronic Interfaces

Category	Commentary
Organization	Field Sales spends non-value administrative time entering information in duplicate systems
Business Processes	Field Sales enters promotions into both internal TPM System and Customer Portals. There are no automated processes.
IT Systems	TPM System 1, TPM System 2, Internal IT System, External System, Customer Portal
Master Data	Deal Sheets, Product Hierarchy, Customer Product Item Code
KPIs	
Change Management	Short term there will be a significant amount of process changes and retraining on existing processes and systems. Long term benefit is very positive.

Recommendation: Develop Electronic Interfaces

Category	Commentary
60-Second Elevator Pitch	Field sales spend non-value administrative time by creating deal sheets and promotions in multiple systems. An electronic interface between systems could automate transaction processes across multiple systems. This would reduce human entry errors and increase the accuracy and speed of deal and promotion entry, payment reconciliation, and completion of promotions. One aspect is the feeds from External System to TPM System 1 could create automate payments greatly reducing manual double entry into multiple systems

Case Conclusion

We received great support from the steering committee.

Once they got their heads around the impact that pricing had on the organization, they agreed that it had been a problem for a while that needed to be fixed. It was not going to be easy, but they were committed to getting the issue corrected.

It would not happen overnight, and it would take a while to implement the changes, but again, it was the right thing to do.

The teams rolled into the implementation with a high level of enthusiasm and support across the organization.

Corrective Actions

Besides pricing, an additional 20 recommendations developed by the project teams were approved by the steering committee.

The recommendations covered organization, business process, information technology, data governance, performance management, policy and controls and change management.

Results

It would take a number of years to completely implement changes to address pricing across the organization.

Of the 20 other recommendations, some were quick hitters while others were mid-term and long-term projects.

The implementation of the changes in a transformation project can take years to see the final results embedded in the organization as standard operating procedures (SOP).

DILOs

Day in the Life of (DILO) Study

A Day In the Life Of (DILO) Study is a tool used in process optimization and transformation to identify work tasks and activities that are not value-added to an individual or group being studied.

Obviously, the objective is to eliminate non-value-added tasks and activities.

DILO roots are based on Lean principles which are geared around minimizing waste and improving productivity.

When I have performed DILO studies, it was always interesting to see the individual's or group's reaction to what I found as non-value-added tasks and activities.

It is the non-biased, objective observations that catch people off guard.

Individuals and groups go through their work tasks and activities which have been developed over time.

They typically don't put much thought into what they do on a daily basis to get their work done.

I have used process flow maps to document the daily activities and tasks and the utilization of The Five Whys to query why a certain activity or task is undertaken.

Of course, you already know the answer to that question: "It's the way we have always done things."

DILO studies do take time, so you have to be ultra-prepared.

But don't just look at one day of activity.

I like to evaluate at least three days of activities as each day can offer a unique set of circumstances.

As discussed before, hidden factories are rampant in business. A well thought out and executed DILO study is a great methodology to identify hidden factories. DILOs also identify institutional and tribal knowledge, which are key to our work as an Archaeologist and Anthropologist.

When you perform a DILO study, you are really solving mysteries around efficient and effective behaviors and cultural norms. As you can imagine, individuals and groups are very sensitive to DILO studies. They think you are trying to pinpoint how bad they are at doing their jobs. DILOs require a proactive approach to change management.

Communication is key with the individuals or groups in the study.

You really need to have developed a very tight scope for the DILO and be able to articulate the objectives to the individuals or group clearly.

I was working on an ERP global design for a manufacturing company where we developed multiple DILOs from the corporate office to the shop floor. Everyone was very sensitive to the DILO work we were performing. We had to explain that we were trying to get a better understanding of their daily work habits so that we could design the enhanced future state processes with the correct technology tools to make them more efficient.

We weren't there to criticize their work but to understand what they did on a daily basis. Still, we had to prove ourselves and justify our approach over and over again as we worked our way through the organization.

At this point, you may be asking, what is the difference between the process flow mapping we discussed in the Mega Mystery and as it pertains to a DILO? In actuality, the DILO means the continuation of decomposing the processes down to level 4.

We identified the level 4 processes on the level 3 process flow maps; now the DILO brings us down to the details inside each level 4 processes.

I have actually done a DILO for a group of products as strange as that may sound.

The manufacturing process for an organization produced a main product and a number of by-products. A by-product is a secondary product derived from a manufacturing process. It can be useful or considered waste. (Bran, is an example is a by-product of the milling of flour.)

The company was blending off the by-products into a number of different main products so that they would not have to dispose of the by-products or classify them as waste.

The company lacked control as to which by-product was going into which main product.

I did a DILO study named a Day In the Life Of a By-Product.

The DILO analysis was eye-opening as I uncovered many uses of the by-products that were unknown and not approved.

The DILO identified the source of a number of quality problems the company was experiencing.

The unapproved use of the by-products in the main products was resulting in performance issues of the main product. Up until that point, the source of the quality issue was unknown.

I have discussed three examples of how a DILO can be used.

- ERP global design
- Level 4 documentation of the business process.
- The Day In the Life of a By-Product.

DILOs are good for identifying hidden factories and institutional and tribal knowledge.

However, be careful concerning the change management issues with DILOs. They can and will rub people the wrong way.

A Few Closing Thoughts on the Process Area

I hope the four project examples of business process optimization and transformation have been helpful in identifying the work required to perform these types of projects.

I hope you can see that there are process optimization and transformation opportunities across an entire organization.

I hope you can see that any process that may be in question is a viable candidate for process optimization and transformation.

I hope you can see that any process needs monitoring and a continuous improvement plan.

These four projects are a small sampling of the optimization and transformation projects I have worked on during my career.

I thought they would be good examples that cut across a variety of business areas.

We wore all of our hats during these four projects:

- **Anthropologist**
- **Archaeologist**
- **Detective**
- **Strategist**
- **Psychologist**
- **Psychiatrist**
- **Conductor**

Process optimization and transformation is the discipline of adjusting a process or processes so as to optimize and transform conditions that lead to the removal of inefficient and ineffective work.

Process optimization and transformation is the discipline of adjusting a process or processes so as to optimize and transform conditions that lead to the removal of inefficient and ineffective work.

When optimizing and transforming a process, the goal is to maximize one or more of the processes. This is done by identifying the critical activities and bottlenecks and putting corrective actions in place.

Process optimization and transformation is an art as well as a science. The work is created with imagination and skill.

What are the skills required to be good at process optimization and transformation?

1. Common sense
2. Inquisitive mind
3. Logical thinking
4. Understanding the big picture
5. Getting into the details
6. Understanding cause and effect relationships
7. Distinguishing between symptoms and root cause(s)
8. Discipline

CHAPTER 5

INFORMATION TECHNOLOGY AND MASTER DATA

I started my education as a data processing major. That's what we called it back in the day: data processing.

I took computer programming classes in BAL (Basic Assembly Language), COBOL (Common Business-Oriented Language) and RPG (Report Program Generator). As a data processing major, we did not have to take Fortran (FORmula TRANslation). That was reserved for the geeky engineers with the pocket protectors and HP 35 calculators.

I excelled at programming but really did not like it. It was too detailed for me.

And I could not type. Period (.), comma (,), semicolon (;) and colon (:) made a world of difference in the program.

I would put our Univac computer into a loop by not putting in the period at the end of a line of code. I guess I had a thing for commas!

I was well-known to the computer operators at my school. The funny part is that I did a work-study in the computer department.

This was the time of punch cards, reel-to-reel tapes and disk packs.

The school I attended required that data processing majors take accounting classes. I found that I enjoyed accounting more than data processing and definitely more than programming. So, I changed my major and finished my degree in accounting.

My first job outside school was in an accounting management training program. We spent six months in a department then rotated to the next assignment. One of my assignments was in the data control department.

The data control department managed the flow of transactions in the corporate computer system such as accounts payable invoices, accounts receivable postings and journal entries.

The most complex part of the job was the monthly close.

Multiple manufacturing plants across the country were required to close their books on the last working day of the month and send the selected financial information to the corporate office.

This, along with closing accounts payable, accounts receivable, fixed assets, general ledger and accruals were all part of the close.

The corporate office was on the East Coast with the furthest plants located in Los Angeles and San Francisco.

We had to wait until those plants submitted their closing data for us to finish the initial closing cycle and run the preliminary reports for the close.

It did not help that they were three hours behind us.

Unfortunately, the Los Angeles plant was disorganized, and some- times we had to wait until one am to get their data. We'd usually go out for dinner, then maybe take a quick nap before Los Angeles sent us their data.

Being on a rotation with no experience, I was managed by a guy named Rich, who had been in the department for three years.

One particular month, Los Angeles was extremely late, and we were not able to finish the initial close until almost 3 am. I was fatigued and blurry-eyed, to say the least.

We ran the preliminary reports and checked a few key fields to make sure the ledgers were in balance. At 4 am, we were flipping through a four-inch stack of green bar computer paper verifying that all the transactions had been properly handled.

Rich and I got to the last balance to verify, and it was a match. It was 4:30 am on Saturday morning, and I was due back in the office by 10 am to complete the close. We would send information to the corporate teams and back to the plants later in the day on this Saturday.

The office was buzzing with us accounting folks on a beautiful Saturday morning when I walked in. As I sat down at my desk, Rich walked up to me. "David, you screwed up the close. Pat wants to see us in her office." Pat was a true accounting professional and one of the best people I have ever worked with and for.

Rich and I sat down, and Pat calmly said that we had missed one of the key fields on the report, which did not balance.

I was shocked as I remembered that though my bleary eyes, everything was in balance.

She put the 4-inch stack of green bar computer paper in front of us and asked us to turn to the page she had marked.

I looked at it and remembered that the number was what we had reconciled to. She, in turn, looked at me and said, "Turn to the next page. "

When I flipped to the next page, there it was, a: $1.5 million variance staring me in the face.

The number we saw was what we were looking for, but we had failed to turn the page where the financial reconciliation was completed.

Oh, this is not good. I had the first sinking feeling of my corporate career at that moment.

As I sat there, stunned, there was a knock-on Pat's door. It was the corporate controller, Alfred, a rather stern older gentleman. My sinking feeling got a whole lot deeper.

"Pat, have you been able to share your finding with David and Rich?" he asked.

"Yes, we were just going over the error," she said.

Alfred and I made eye contact, and he asked, "What do you have to say for yourself?"

But I could not really talk. I thought I was going to get fired from my first job.

Then, Pat, Alfred and Rich looked at each other and smiled.

What are you smiling about?

Pat turned to me and said. "David, you were set up. This is part of your training."

I still couldn't talk and was just listening.

Pat explained: "You see, Rich had turned the page and knew that the numbers did not balance. They are not supposed to. Every month we put in a phantom entry with a known amount that is part of our reconciliation process. If that known amount does not show up exactly where it is expected, we know we have a problem. He saw the exact phantom number and knew the processes had completed correctly." Pat paused for a moment and leaned forward over her desk as she continued, "You are off the hook but not entirely because you did fail to turn the page and catch the out-of-balance situation."

Again, no words came forth from my mouth.

"So, lesson learned?" she asked.

"Yes, ma'am," I replied, finally able to speak.

I share this story with you because this was my first exposure to a big corporate "data processing" system. This learning experience has stayed with me my entire career. Thanks, Alfred, Pat and Rich for an early lesson in data governance and controls!

Over the years, I have been involved in a wide variety of technology transformation solutions from ERP systems such SAP, Oracle, JDE and BPCS to Edge Solutions in supply chain, regulatory, performance management and even two proprietary business systems.

I led the teams that ideated, designed, developed and implemented the proprietary business systems. I have a real soft spot in my heart for these solutions. I enjoy building software solutions. It's where I can blend my business with my information technology background.

In today's world, it is hard to imagine that there is not an opportunity with the information technology platform in an optimization or transformation project. Technology solutions drive operational and process performance efficiencies.

In this section, I will discuss some of my experiences, implementation methodology improvements and my favorite pet peeves in information technology.

Pet Peeve #1, Technology Consultants with No Business/ Domain Experience

I cannot tell you how often I have seen companies deploy technology consultants on complex system implementations when the consultants knew next to nothing about business.

I have worked across multiple industries in a variety of disciplines.

Through the years, I have learned that there are some basic operational problems that are shared across industries whether it is in product development, marketing, sales, supply chain and operations or finance.

Of course, there are nuances in different industries, but time to market, campaigns, growth, agility, utilization and product costing are replicated across all the industries I have worked in during my career.

I'm not saying every technology consultant needs this level of business acumen, but you would think a consultant implementing a demand planning solution would have real experience in demand planning.

I have seen the lack of business acumen or domain knowledge on a variety of implementations.

I have experienced my peeve on implementations where the technology consultant configuring the systems does not understand the business/domain ramifications or impacts of the settings.

It is extremely important that the system settings are configured properly to align with the business requirements of the solution. Understanding the business requirements is the key.

Typically, you start seeing the disconnects in early beta testing. Functional documentation for the implementation lacks some of the unique business requirements.

I have audited implementations where an experienced business/domain consultant would have caught the problem.

We'll do a thorough investigation with the client to uncover missed functional requirements.

Many times, the implementation can be delayed as the consultants have to redo some of the configurations.

If you are implementing say SAP software, these requirements should have been flushed out during the SAP implementation step Business Blueprinting.

But in these cases, the technology consultants did not know the right questions to ask or did not understand the ramifications of the answers they were given.

The moral of the story: when you are interviewing consultants for an implementation, it is more than critical that the company have business-knowledgeable consultants on the project to be able to translate the business requirements to the technology consultants. As well, the business-knowledgeable consultants need to stay with the project for some duration.

I had just joined a company in an executive leadership position when I was asked to visit a project ASAP because there were some significant startup issues that needed to be addressed immediately.

It was my third week on the job, and I was headed to a global client. But I got problems.

We had a meeting set up with the client project manager and their cross-functional team.

Before our meeting with the client, I connected with our project manager to get an update as to the status of the project and the issues they were facing.

"What is the biggest issue with the client right now?" I asked.

"They don't like us," replied our project manager.

"OK, they don't like us. Can you be a little more specific?

"They believe that our team will not be able to deliver the solution based on the makeup of our team."

"What is it about the makeup of our team that they don't like?" I prodded.

"The number one issue is that we don't have a domain specialist on our team. We are all technologists. That said, we have implemented at a number of clients' locations and have learned a lot about domains."

"Well, that does appear to be a gap on the team. Is this normal?" I questioned.

"Yes, our domain team is part of the sales process, but they don't come onsite for the implementations."

"Interesting, and why is that?"

"They don't like to travel overnight too often."

I nodded in acknowledgment and wondered what I had gotten myself into.

We continued our meeting, and I learned some additional interesting facts about our implementation methodologies.

The next morning our project manager and I met with the client project manager and their cross-functional implementation team.

After some pleasantries through the introductions, the PM got down to business pretty quickly and pointedly.

"Our team does not have confidence in your implementation team," the project manager stated. "The solution we bought is to manage complex global requirements across our business platforms. When our team talks to your team, there is no one on your team who truly understands the global landscape. Yes, we admit that we have some unique requirements. However, a knowledgeable industry professional would be able to answer our team's questions without having to research every detail. We are not happy with the team and have made that known to our leadership. We have been waiting for your visit to discuss our path forward." And that was that.

Choosing my words carefully, I replied, "As you know, I have just joined the company and have made your project my Number 1 priority. I will be meeting with our team this week, and I will discuss your concerns. I will get back to you within a week as to what will be a suitable path forward. My team has advised that they can continue with parts of the implementation. I will ask for you and your team to engage with our team as we work toward resolution."

"For the time being, that will be an acceptable approach. But I caution you that if we do not receive a suitable path forward, we will shut down the project," the PM advised.

After talking with our domain and technical teams, we came up with an acceptable path forward for the client. This included partnering a member of our local domain team with a member of our corporate team who had broader global knowledge of the requirements.

I updated our CEO and leadership team concerning our proposed path forward and received their approval to continue.

When we presented the revised domain team concept to the client, they said that was what they were expecting.

I made another trip to the client two weeks later with our domain team onsite. We had an excellent meeting with the client team. They were impressed with the local knowledge as well as the global knowledge of our corporate specialist.

The local and corporate domain specialist would alternate onsite so that we had 100% coverage on critical design, development and the testing stages of the project.

Yes, it did cost us some additional money with the corporate specialist, but that was a minor investment when looking at client satisfaction and the value of the project.

Going forward, we built in one or two domain specialists for the define and design stages that were onsite. During the development and testing stages of the implementations, we did a combination of remote and onsite domain specialists.

All hands were on deck for project Go Live, with a combination of remote and onsite for post Go Live support.

The point is that the solution provider has to have domain specialists on the project, whether in CRM, marketing, supply chain, operations, or a regulatory solution.

Pet Peeve #2, Master Data

When most people think about master data, their minds go to corporate master, customer master, supplier master and item master. These are the foundational master data elements. These are the ERP master data elements.

When you get past the foundational master data elements, the complexity of other master data increases exponentially. And many have a challenge managing the basics.

Let's take a look at master data for manufacturing, maintenance and warehouse management.

In manufacturing, most companies have multiple manufacturing departments making components of the finished product. They will have multiple pieces of equipment in each department across the organization.

The amount and criticality of master data required to set up the manufacturing module of today's systems is enormous.

From my experience, most companies do not have the data required to populate the manufacturing master data accurately. Bills of materials (BOMs), the parts needed to make the component, and the routings (how the components flow through the department) along with machines settings are all part of master data for the manufacturing module.

Manufacturing master data is a great example of tribal knowledge. The machine operators know that to run this particular component, the speed of the line needs to be "this setting," and the tension setting needs to be "that setting," and if the line goes any faster for this particular component, quality goes down the tubes.

Now multiply this across a plant that makes 50 finished goods, across 10 operations with 200 machines, and you can see the extent of the master data required to set up the manufacturing systems. Obviously, 50 finished goods is a low number of products.

Even if the plant has manufacturing engineers, I have found that they don't have accurate manufacturing master data. Accurate and up-to-date BOMs and routings have occupied a particular gap in the implementations I have been a part of in manufacturing. Forget about the machine settings.

Computerized maintenance management systems (CMMS) or asset management systems (AMS) are designed to act as repository and transaction systems that contain information about your assets and maintenance activities to support predictive maintenance.

Predictive Maintenance, one of the big buzzes in consulting around artificial intelligence (AI) and machine learning (ML), helps organizations assess assets, diagnose problems using monitoring tools like sensors and image analytics, design the appropriate solution leveraging advanced algorithms and machine-learning principles and deploy sustainable and repeatable maintenance solutions and an optimized asset lifecycle maintenance plan.

These systems have HUGE master data requirements. Think about mapping every piece of equipment in a manufacturing plant, the maintenance schedules, and all the parts and suppliers that support the equipment.

A warehouse management system (WMS) comprises software and processes that allow organizations to control and administer warehouse operations from the time goods or materials enter a warehouse until they move out.[25]

Picking, receiving, storage and inventory management, counting, warehouse controls, lot and serial tracking, order allocation, wave planning and segregated materials are all components of a WMS that require master data such as business rules. The WMS runs off of the business rules.

The master data challenge is what I have seen on the multiple technology implementations across a variety of clients and industries.

Master data is the Achilles heel of any implementation, and companies are not prepared for the data requirements.

And this is just to set up the systems. We haven't even started discussing the daily updates and maintenance of the data.

This is the huge part of the data governance of master data. Because if the data is not correct, the systems whether they are ERP, manufacturing, maintenance, or warehouse management will give you incorrect instructions and compromise decisions. This can result in a classic example of people losing confidence in the new technology solution and going back to their old manual ways. The hidden factories start to reappear here — that's if they ever went away in the first place. The quality and accuracy of the master data for these kinds of systems are extensive and critical as to how the systems operate, and the user acceptance.

Industry 4.0 — which relates to the deployment of artificial intelligence, machine learning, robotic process automation, internet of things (IoT), industrial internet of things (IIoT) and cloud computing — has huge master data requirements.

Data Governance

Creating and maintaining master data in ERP or in any technology system requires a lot of discipline. SAP, Oracle, Microsoft and others all have very stringent requirements concerning master data. If a company is new to master data at these levels, the task can feel daunting.

Detailed below is the master data model for the core master data elements for customer, material, vendor, processing, manufacturing and transportation. This is the foundation for master data in a manufacturing implementation.

Integrated Master Data Setup Overview

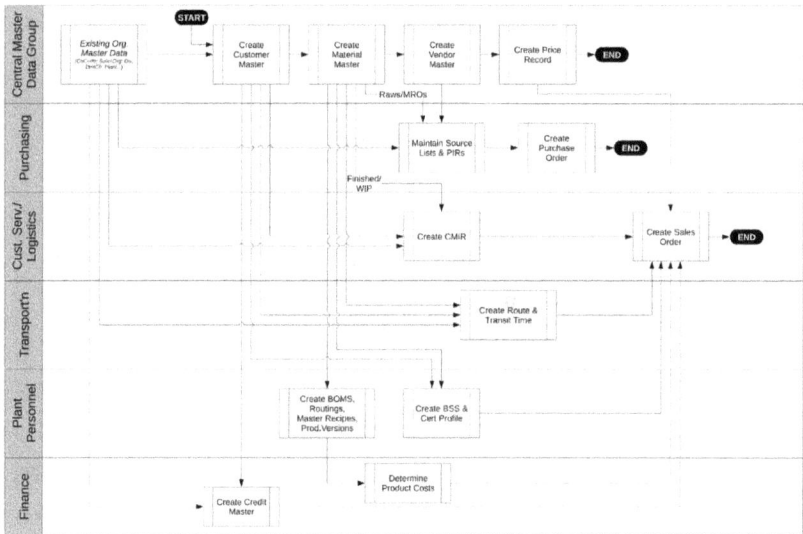

There are a number of business scenarios that require parts of each element to "set up a new customer with a new product" or "set up a new customer with an existing product." The examples below show color-coded boxes in green to identify what exactly is needed to populate for the particular "setup."

Integrated Master Data Setup – New Customer/ New Product w/New Raw Materials

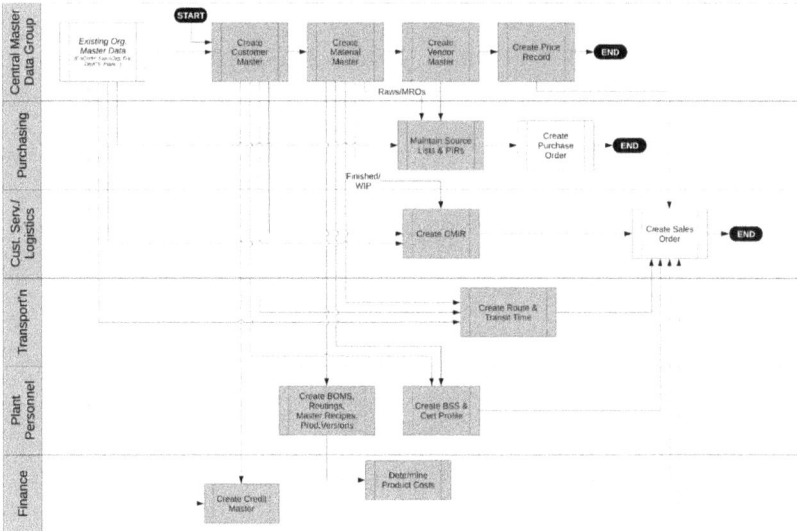

Integrated Master Data Setup – New Customer/ New Product w/Existing Raw Materials

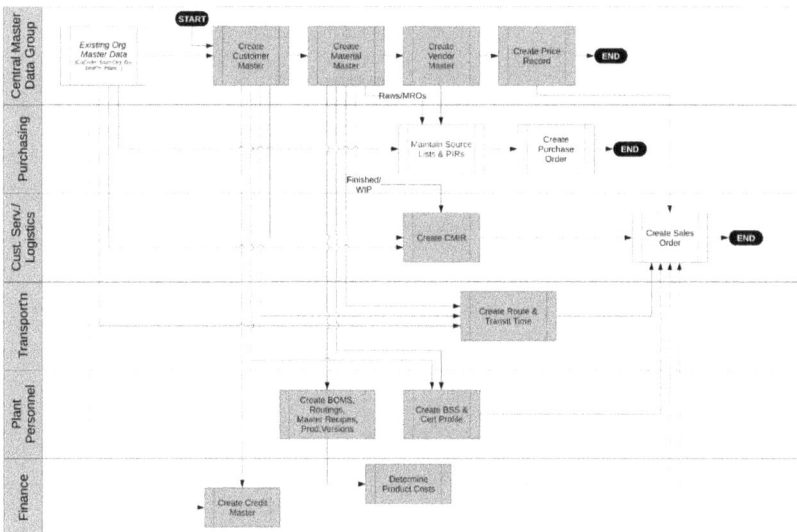

Integrated Master Data Setup – New Customer/Existing Product

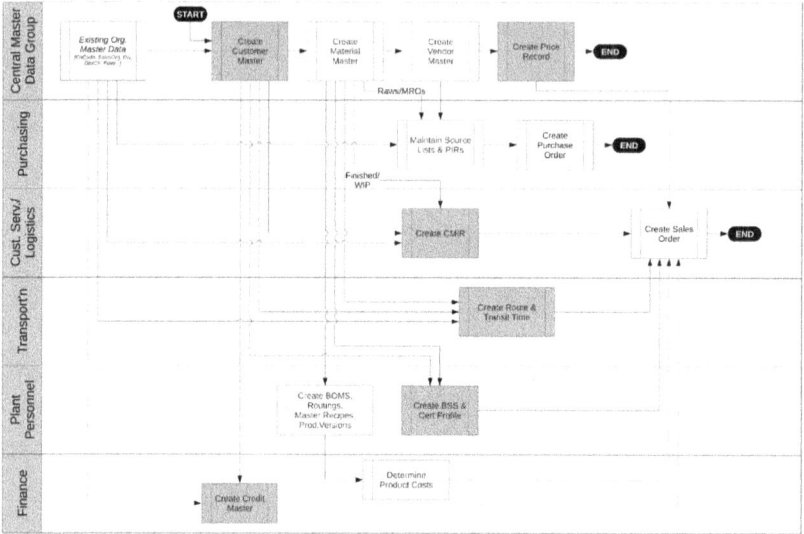

Shifting away from the customer, let's look at another plant with new or existing products.

Integrated Master Data Setup – New Plant w/New and Existing Product

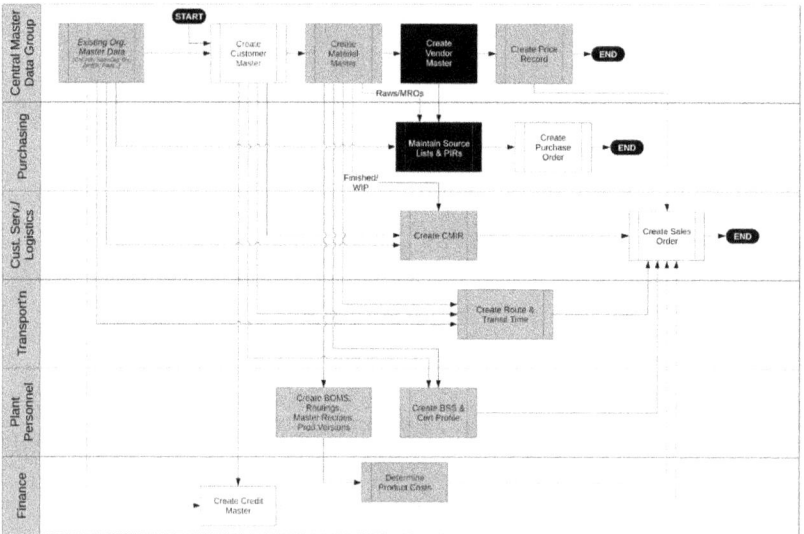

A colleague and I were discussing how we could make master data governance a more robust and methodology-driven management system.

As two Six Sigma Black Belts, our idea was: Six Sigma for master data.

The methodology follows the Six Sigma approach: define, measure, analyze, improve, control (DMAIC).

This is a perfect methodology for master data governance.

Six Sigma Master Data Approach

1. **Define**
   - Master Data Organization
   - Master Data Business Processes
   - Master Data Information Technology
   - Master Data Elements

2. **Measure**
    - Master Data Organization KPIs / Metrics
    - Master Data Business Processes KPIs / Metrics
    - Master Data Information Technology KPIs / Metrics
    - Master Data Elements KPIs / Metrics

3. **Analyze**
    - Master Data Organization KPIs / Metrics
    - Master Data Business Processes KPIs / Metrics
    - Master Data Information Technology KPIs / Metrics
    - Master Data Elements KPIs / Metrics

4. **Improve**
    - Master Data Organization on Continuous Improvement Plans
    - Master Data Business Processes Continuous Improvement Plans
    - Master Data Information Technology Continuous Improvement Plans
    - Master Data Elements Continuous Improvement Plans

5. **Control**
    - Master Data Organization Governance
    - Master Data Business Processes Governance
    - Master Data Information Technology Governance
    - Master Data Elements Governance

Let me offer an observation. Some people get uncomfortable when you mention Six Sigma because they believe Six Sigma is too complicated and they believe they have to be a Black Belt to understand it. The point I will make is that it is called Six Sigma for master data. But you don't have to be a Six Sigma Black Belt to make it a robust master data governance management system based on the DMAIC process. Take the words Six Sigma out of the description, and you have a master data governance management system.

If your organization does not have a strong master data governance management system, you are asking for and living with data problems every day. You can see from the previous examples how many systems require master data, and if there is no governance or continuous improvement system in place, your data is going to be crap. All you will hear are complaints.

> **If your organization does not have a strong master data governance management system, you are asking for and living with data problems every day.**

Now with the added complexity of a Cloud platform, The Internet of Things (IoT) and the resulting Big Data, the need for a structured MDM methodology is not critical but paramount.

MDM technology suppliers are racing to keep up with the ever-evolving needs of controlling master data. Advances in ML and AI are all being touted as evolutionary in MDM governance. But any article you read still discusses the requirements for a methodology around the governance of master data supported by the implementation of these advancing technologies.

Another Master Data Example

One terminology commonly used today is Edge Application.

Edge Application is a software system that connects to an ERP system. It has its own master data requirements, plus it needs to utilize master data from the ERP.

The software system in question is a very common technology solution used across a wide variety of industries. The system is integrated into multiple modules of the ERP, so there are a number of interfaces to maintain and an extensive amount of master data to validate.

The software system requires very accurate master data for the product, manufacturing processes and business rules that govern how the system behaves.

Business rules are master data, but they are also policies that relate to settings.

The system, when integrated into the ERP system, retrieves a variety of master data elements from the modules. The system then creates its own master data as part of its processing system and sends that master data back to the ERP modules.

The team dedicated to the implementation of this solution found that the existing master data elements were outdated and inaccurate. Certain master data elements had not been updated in years.

The implementation team had to go through the painstaking process of multiple data validation cycles to verify the accuracy of the master data. They had to get down to a very low level of granularity to validate all the different master data elements.

The data cleansing of the master data took a long time and used a significant amount of resources.

There are so many lessons to be learned.

Here are two of them.

Unfortunately, the master data elements had not been maintained and updated for years.

If you think about Six Sigma for master data, "improve" is the fourth step of the process.

Lesson 1: If the company had put a structured master data governance process in place, they would have been improving the accuracy and quality of their master data elements as part of a continuous improvement program.

Lesson 2: Do you know where most of this master data information resided? You guessed it. It was both institutional knowledge but mostly tribal knowledge of different team members. The team had to "pick the brain" of so many people to get the master data elements correct.

Pet Peeve #3, Smart/Intelligent Numbers vs. Non-Smart/ Non-Intelligent Numbers

I am not going to get into the debate about smart/intelligent numbers vs. non-smart/non-intelligent numbers.

A smart/intelligent number in this business context is the item number for a raw material or finished good. The number is actually a code that explains characteristic of the raw material or finished good.

As an example: 012.563.774.213206 where 012 is the country code, 563 is the state or province code, 774 is the plant number, 213206 is the number where 21 identifies it as an electronic part and 3206 is the actual part number.

A non-smart/non-intelligent number is a randomly system-generated item number. As an example, 012.563.774.213206 means nothing if it has no context. It's just a code number.

I will only explain what I have seen when a company converts from smart/intelligent numbers to non-smart/non-intelligent numbers.

Many companies have a very elaborate smart/intelligent numbering system.

Ask anyone in customer service or manufacturing what kind of finished product they put out, and they will rattle off a model size, material and color right off the top of their heads by just looking at the finished goods part number.

Now, with the implementation of a new or upgraded ERP, the company is going to a non-smart, randomly generated, finished goods part number.

As an example:

> Everyone on the project team and end users are well aware that this huge change from smart number to non-smart number is happening in the project.
>
> We are at the phase of the project where we are to begin User Acceptance Testing (UAT).
>
> User Acceptance Testing is the final verification that the solution works for those who will be the "users" of the solution.
>
> And so UAT begins and the follow conversation happens between a "user" and a project team member.
>
> "What the hell are these finished goods part numbers? They make no sense."
>
> "We've been telling you from the beginning of the project that we are getting away from your smart numbers and are going to non-smart numbers."

"Well, that is just not acceptable."

"Let's see how it goes with UAT."

Chaos!

UAT falls flat on its face.

My recommendation is that if you have plans to go from smart/intelligent numbers to non-smart/non-intelligent numbers, you better plan early and educate.

This change from smart/intelligent numbers to non-smart/non-intelligent numbers can and will derail a project fast.

These numbers are ingrained in people's minds.

When you throw the non-smart/non-intelligent numbers in front of the users it is like you are asking them to learn a foreign language or how to code.

If your organization is going from smart/intelligent numbers to non-smart/non-intelligent numbers, take the time to expose the users to the concept of non-smart/non-intelligent numbers before the system is in user acceptance training (UAT).

Educate, educate, educate the user population.

 **Educate, educate, educate the user population.**

Determine how the users are understanding and comprehending the change from smart to non-smart numbers.

Because UAT is typically near the end of the implementation process, it will be too late by then to try to educate the users and to determine their comprehension of the change.

Point blank, it is not going to be easy for people to get the change from smart to non-smart numbers.

Be ready for disruption at Go Live even if you have done upfront education and training.

When you press the Go Live switch, the real-world hits, orders have to be processed, and product manufactured and shipped. So, hold on for a possible wild ride.

Pet Peeve #4, Pareto's Principle of Software

Let's talk about "Putting the Right Person in the Right Seat."

When I was with Oracle, I was exposed to some of the emerging technologies right around the time the internet was exploding with huge advances in the complexity of these solutions.

I had come from an organization where the Business Planning and Control System (BPCS) was our ERP system.

BPCS, from System Software Associates (SSA), sits on an IBM AS 400 platform and was focused on manufacturing and distribution companies.

It was very popular, with over 8,000 implementations worldwide. BPCS's heyday was in the 1980s and early 1990s. SSA ultimately sold out to Infor.

BPCS was a very good blocking-and-tackling system. It had a wide range of modules, and it was a good solution for mid-size companies.

My experience with state-of-the-art ERP systems at that time was limited.

When I got to Oracle, I was shown the 11i E-Business Suite, one of the first web-based platforms.

Wow! I was blown away by the technology.

But it gets better. Then I am shown Demand Planner, based on the Oracle Express multi-dimensional database and Advanced Supply Chain Planner (ASCP). This is what is now called Edge Solutions.

What the fudge is this ASCP?

I am not in Kansas anymore.

These systems are amazingly powerful and complex.

I'm not sure where this came from and even why I thought of it, but I developed "Pareto's Principle of Software."

I'll explain Pareto's Principle of Software in more detail below, but first an intro- duction to Vilfredo Federico Damaso Pareto. Pareto was an Italian engineer, sociologist, economist, political scien- tist and philosopher. He introduced the concept of "Pareto Efficiency" and helped develop the field of microeconomics.

He was also the first to discover that income follows a "Pareto Distribution," which is a power law of

probability distribution. The "Pareto Principle" was named after him, and it was built on the observation that 80% of the land in Italy was owned by about 20% of the population.

The 80/20 Rule, or Pareto Principle, is a foundation principle I see play out on every project. As an example:

- 80% of sales come from 20% of the customers.
- 80% of sales come from 20% of the products.
- 80% of profits come from 20% of the products.
- 80% of inventory comes from 20% of the products.

> The Pareto Principle is a foundation principle I see play out on every project.

My Pareto Principle of Software:

- 80% of the users will use 20% of the software's capabilities.
- 20% of the users may use 80% of the software's capabilities. (Maybe!)
- Nobody uses the top 20% of the software's capabilities, but that is what software companies demonstrate during the selling process!

Certain types of software require individuals with more advanced analytical skills. If the organization tries to force-fit an individual into a position running a solution that requires advanced analytical skills that person does not have, this is a recipe for disaster.

I've seen this a number of times on projects. We'll guide the client in this area and then they select someone who obviously does not have the skills. They tell us, "Oh, they'll grow into the position." In most cases they do not grow into the position.

The company has now delayed getting value from the solution, potentially caused operational issues, and frustrated or even humiliated an individual.

I personally would be hard-pressed to operate some of these advanced solutions.

You have to put "The Right Person in the Right Seat" when it comes to operating these solutions.

And companies need to be creative.

You may have to hire outside talent and think differently.

Many plants are away from metropolitan areas.

I have seen companies set up shuttles to bring the more educated staff in from the local metropolitan area. Of course, there is a cost to run the shuttles, but the cost/benefit analysis supports establishing the shuttles program.

Another option is with a local college or university. Work Study Programs and college recruiting has worked for a number of companies. Developing a relationship with a college or university will provide your organization young professionals who are eager to learn in a real-world environment.

Also, these solutions can be run from a centralized location, like the corporate or divisional office. When centralized, an individual can run the solution across multiple facilities and, honestly, around the globe.

The point is that organizations need to put "The Right Person in the Right Seat" and may need to be creative in the process.

Pet Peeve #5, Lack of Process Documentation

By now, you've most likely gotten the feeling that I like structure and processes. If you have not gotten that drift yet, well it's got to be my fault.

What I have seen over and over again, and I have fallen into this trap, too, is that there is not enough process and workflow documentation when implementing a new technology.

But before we start in with my fifth pet peeve, let's discuss the difference between "educate" and "train."

Because "educate" and "train" are very different, and people get them confused.

Educate:

- To provide with information
- To persuade or condition to feel, believe, or act in a desired way
- To develop mentally, morally, or aesthetically especially by instruction

Train:

- To teach so as to make fit, qualified, or proficient
- To form by instruction, discipline, or drill

You need first to educate your audience to make them understand. They need to understand why the company is putting in a new software system and the associated benefits to "them" first and then the organization. Because during the education process, the first question people in the organization will ask is, "What's in it for me?" Educating is a critical step in organizational change management.

Training is about learning the tasks required to operate the software. You are not educating. Now, you are training and teaching.

If your employee population doesn't get the full context of the discussion during the education session, it is very difficult to proceed to training.

Skills assessment during training is critical because you don't want to put people into a situation where they can fail.

Let's take a look at an example of some process documentation work from a project.

I was asked to work with an ERP implementation team on developing a more robust set of process documents to support education and training.

We put together a 3-person team to enhance the process documentation.

Together we visited a few plants to first listen to the client about their concerns and to start the education process with the plant teams.

Two of the larger, more complex sites were in close proximity to each other, so we hit them early in the week before we headed to the third plant.

At the end of the visit to the second plant, we were down in the hotel bar having a few drinks and reflecting on our plant visits, the status of the project and what we needed to do going forward.

We asked the bartender for a pen and piece of paper and began to scratch out the ERP end-to-end manufacturing process.

Over the next week, the three us got together and built-in Visio, the ERP end-to-end manufacturing process.

We built the documentation to cover both process and discrete manufacturing. The diagram on page 188 is end-to-end for process manufacturing.

Let me say that these generic models can be easily customized for SAP, Oracle, JDE, Infor, or any other ERP system.

The diagram on page 189 is the planning function for process manufacturing.

The diagram on page 190 depicts end-to-end for discrete marketing.

In planning for discrete manufacturing, you'll see some additional steps in the planning for process vs. discrete in the diagram on page 191.

Finally, please review the chart illustrating the manufacturing and quality for discrete manufacturing on page 192.

Each box is either a visual read of information or a transaction.

Here is the translation:

- A picture of a computer monitor shows that the person handling the transaction needed to view the system.
- The keyboard represents entering data or the progress of a transaction.
- The flash shows the ERP working in the background.
- The barcode picture indicates a barcode transaction was required.
- A picture of a report shows a report would be generated at that transaction step.

We set up multiple education sessions with the client teams, both at the corporate office and out in the plants. Remember we have to start with education!

The education session went well, relieving some of the anxiety people had with the new system. Seeing the end-to-end process visually and then diving down into individual job functions went a long way in building additional trust with the client. At this point, this client knew what they were up against.

Our training team loved what we had put together. It was going to make their lives a whole lot simpler.

As I mentioned, these particular flows can be customized for SAP, Oracle, JDE, Infor or any other ERP.

We were proud that we could get the entire end to end manufacturing ·process on a single Visio process map.

Documenting the transaction steps in technology implementa-tions has turned out to be both a valuable education as well as a training tool.

Due to the fact that users can see the entire end-to-end flow of the software and how it all integrates, we have created an education moment. This is important because the users will see there are upstream and downstream dependencies for the transactions to flow smoothly through the system.

As an example, if a manufacturing work order is not transacted in the system, the product will not be put into inventory, and the system will not allow the order to be shipped.

With this method, the user can visually see all the transactions in their area of responsibility.

When it is time for training, the trainers can use the same flow charts and incorporate them into the training materials.

Process Manufacturing Process Flow

Demand and Production Planning

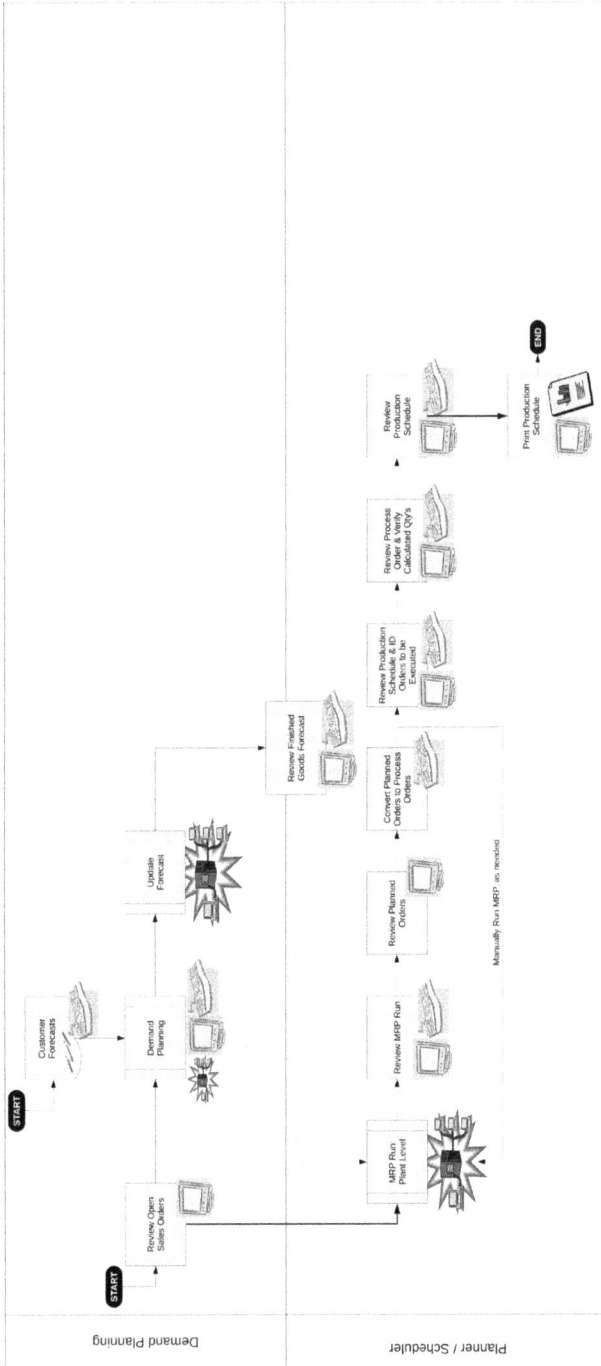

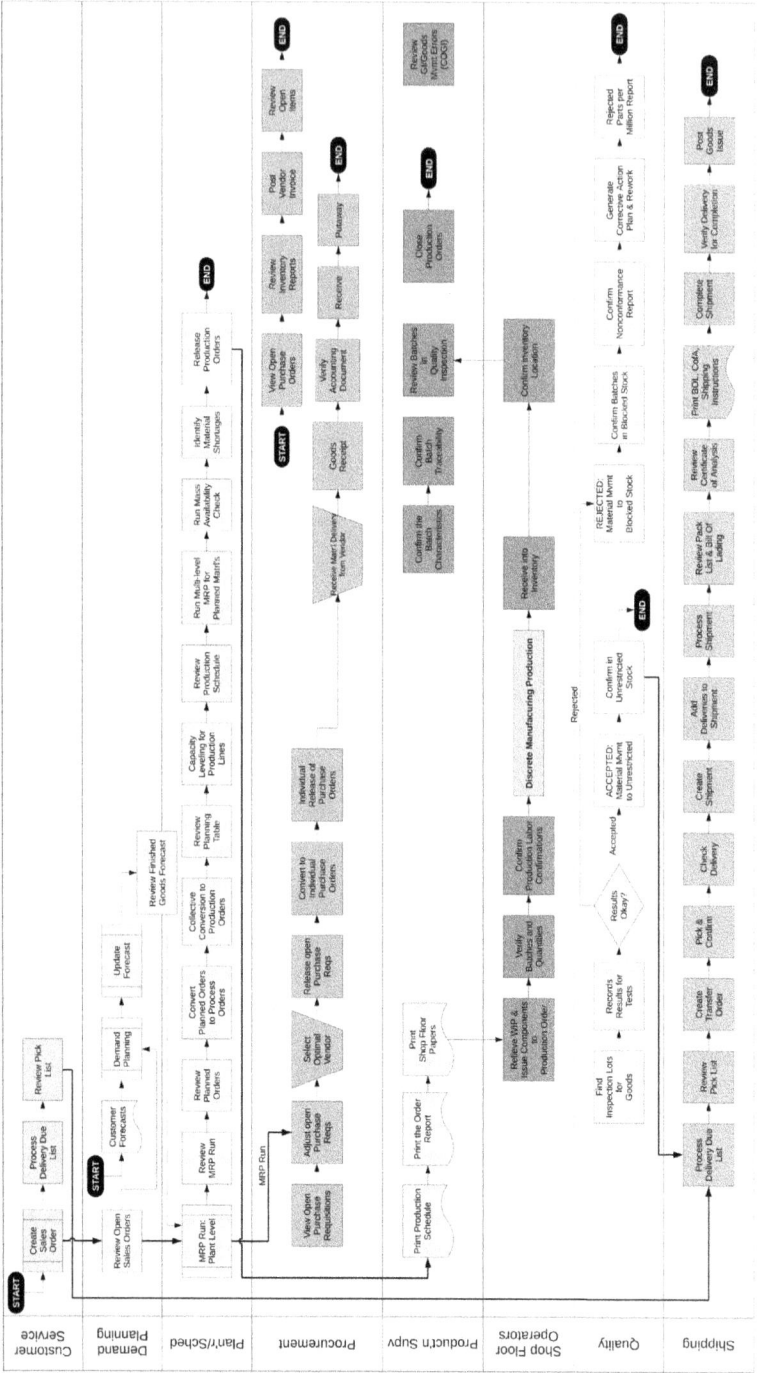

Discrete Manufacturing Process Flow

Demand and Production Planning Discrete

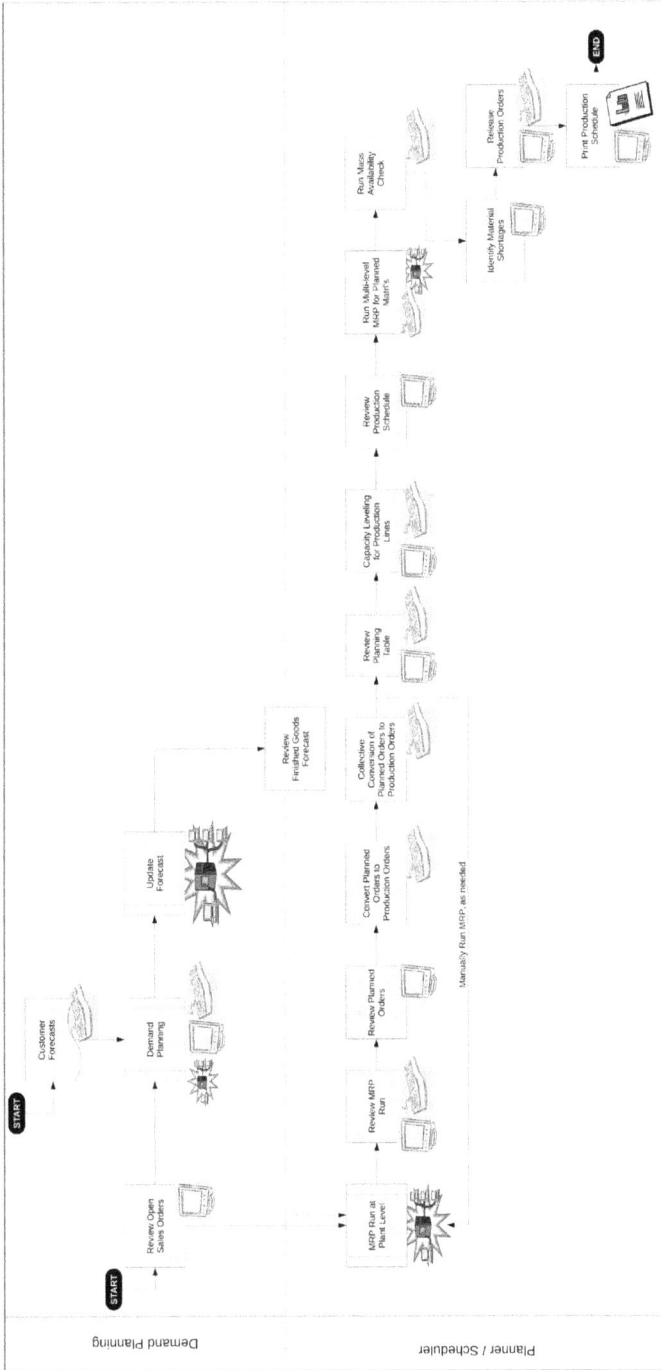

START

Review Open Sales Orders

Customer Forecasts

Demand Planning

Update Forecast

Review Finished Goods Forecast

START

MRP Run at Plant Level

Review MRP Run

Review Planned Orders

Convert Planned Orders to Production Orders

Collective Conversion of Planned Orders to Production Orders

Review Planning Table

Capacity Levelling for Production Lines

Review Production Schedule

Run Multi-level MRP for Planned Matl's

Run Mass Availability Check

Identify Material Shortages

Release Production Orders

Print Production Schedule

Manually Run MRP as needed

END

Demand Planning

Planner / Scheduler

Manufacturing & Quality – Discrete Manufacturing

So, you get a double bang for your buck, when you use education and training.

And the users will not be able to tell you that they don't understand how the system works as you have first educated, and then trained them on the integrated flows of the systems as it relates to specific knowledge about their area of work.

I'm done with my pet peeves now, let's move on to software selection.

Software Selection

I have been part of several optimization and transformation projects where new software was a critical component of the project.

Selecting the right software for your business is one of the most important decisions an organization will make. If you don't include the users and make the selection a C-suite decision, the implementation will be that much more difficult.

Get help. There are some excellent consultants that will help you with the selection process. Make sure they are very knowledgeable about the domain. Meaning, if your organization is in the market for a demand planning solution, make sure the consultant is current with the suppliers of demand planning solutions.

As an example, Gartner is an excellent resource to guide your organization through the software selection process.[27] They produce research called The Magic Quadrant, which is a competitive graphical positioning of the four types of technology providers in fast-growing markets: leaders, visionaries, niche players and challengers. As companion research, Gartner Critical Capabilities notes provide deeper insight into the capability and suitability of providers' IT products and services based on specific or customized use cases.

I advise setting up a cross-functional team of users to be a part of the selection process.

I have mentioned and will go into more details about change champions in the change management section.

Establishing level-1 change champions as members of the cross-functional team will serve three objectives.

1. Get the change champions identified
2. Start the education process with the change champions
3. Build the change champion's influence as early in the journey as possible from selection to implementation.

The next step is the most critical. You must know your requirements.

With the help of the consultant and cross-functional team, document and know your requirements.

For an ERP implementation, I worked closely with a cross-functional team to document their current state processes.

Through this documentation process, using the 5 Whys and the color-coding of processes and transactions, we were able to identify a number of major constraints in their processes.

We identified there was a real need for an additional technology component that was not initially part of the system architecture.

After everything was documented, we built the business case for the additional technology which was presented to the steering committee. Although it was going to cost some additional money, we were able to identify a solution to solve some chronic problems.

A number of these issues were not known before we started decomposing the processes and identifying process constraints.

After we did this, we had a better understanding of the process challenges and the required technology solutions and architecture required to deliver accelerated value.

You should not be afraid to spend the time and money to vet the software selection process thoroughly. The organization is going to live with the decision for many years to come, so you better get it right.

The three critical areas for software selection are:

- Get help
- Establish a cross-functional team
- Know your requirements

The Cloud

Cloud Computing

The Cloud is everywhere these days. It's hard to go a day without seeing a commercial by one of the major cloud-computing providers.

Amazon Web Services (AWS) is the largest and maybe the best-known cloud computing vendor.

But let us not forget about IBM Cloud, Microsoft Azure, Oracle Cloud and SAP Cloud.

Salesforce.com is a cloud-based software company. They provide Software as a Service or SaaS.

SaaS makes up one of three main categories of cloud computing, the others being Infrastructure as a service, IaaS and Platform as a Service, PaaS.

The term for a non-cloud environment is On-Premise.

My first exposure to cloud-computing was back in 2000 when two executives left Oracle (where I was working at the time) to start an ERP Cloud company.

That was a new one on me.

Larry Ellison, CEO of Oracle, had already invested in NetLedger in 1998. NetLedger became known as NetSuite and was acquired by Oracle in 2016.

My first hands-on exposure to a SaaS was when I was with 3E Company back in 2004. 3E provided a SaaS for material safety data sheets (MSDS).

Cloud computing has been around for some time, but the visibility has really accelerated over the past five years.

If you are the owner of an iPhone, MacBook, or iMac, you most likely use iCloud.

Many software vendors are now only offering their solutions as cloud-based; there are no more On-Premise. A good portion of these software vendors use AWS to host their applications.

In the Enterprise space, the ERP migration from SAP ECC to SAP S/4 HANA is a huge shift for many companies to the Cloud.

The deployment models for S/4HANA Finance or full S/4HANA Enterprise Management are Cloud – SaaS, HEC (Hybrid Enterprise

Cloud) — IaaS or On-Premise. The path to a S/4HANA migration and a digital future is complex.

This is a great opportunity for business process optimization and transformation. Companies don't implement ERP systems all the time. System integrators who implement SAP would be doing their clients an injustice if they did not incorporate the opportunity for business process optimization and transformation.

We know that over time, say in the past 10 years, many companies have not incorporated continuous improvement programs to enhance the performance of their ERP systems. It is usually quite the opposite, as processes have deteriorated, and hidden factories have multiplied.

Will business process optimization and transformation take some time? Of course, the answer is yes! But as is the case with any business process optimization and transformation initiative, the benefits must be weighed against the time and the cost.

One of the next phases of cloud computing is serverless cloud.

Serverless is a version of computing in which business logic functions execute on servers that are not your servers; the Cloud provider provides the infrastructure which executes the functions.

Some of the benefits besides reduced costs are scalability, shorter development and deployment times, and improved security.[28]

CHAPTER 6

PERFORMANCE MANAGEMENT AND OPERATIONAL DATA

Business Case for Change

In a previous section, we discussed the charter, which allows for some high-level project goals in growth, savings and investments.

In my favorite project, "Mega Mystery," I introduced a brief discussion on a business case for change.

As the project flows from current state/as-is to root cause analysis to future state design, you are going to be asked for a business case for change.

The business case for change will include the factual evidence you uncovered during the current state documentation and root cause analysis and will include what changes are required to support resolving the root cause.

You will want to use the factual evidence along with forecasted revenue growth, and savings and operational efficiencies along with any investments required to build out the business case for change.

Detailed below are the charts used for presenting the business case for change to the steering committee.

Example: Project Themes for Success

- A new sustainable XXXXXX process is an absolute requirement for us to achieve our strategic growth vision.

- We must educate and train our teams to support a new world class XXXXXX process. Roles & Responsibilities will be clearly defined so that we as an organization are all on the same page.

- The new XXXXXX process must be designed to allow us to execute with the flexibility needed to support our various global businesses. This flexibility will enable our team to effectively manage YYYYYY.

- The decisions resulting from the new XXXXXX process must be quantifiable and fact based. The organization must work from "One Version of the Truth".

- The new XXXXXX process is a Bold change management initiative as we transform our organization into a global leader.

- The Leadership Team will lead by example as we all must embrace the change for the collective good of our individual stakeholders and the organization.

- The new XXXXXX process must be viewed as a competitive advantage for our strategic growth, not as a barrier or hindrance to our success.

Example: Financial Targets

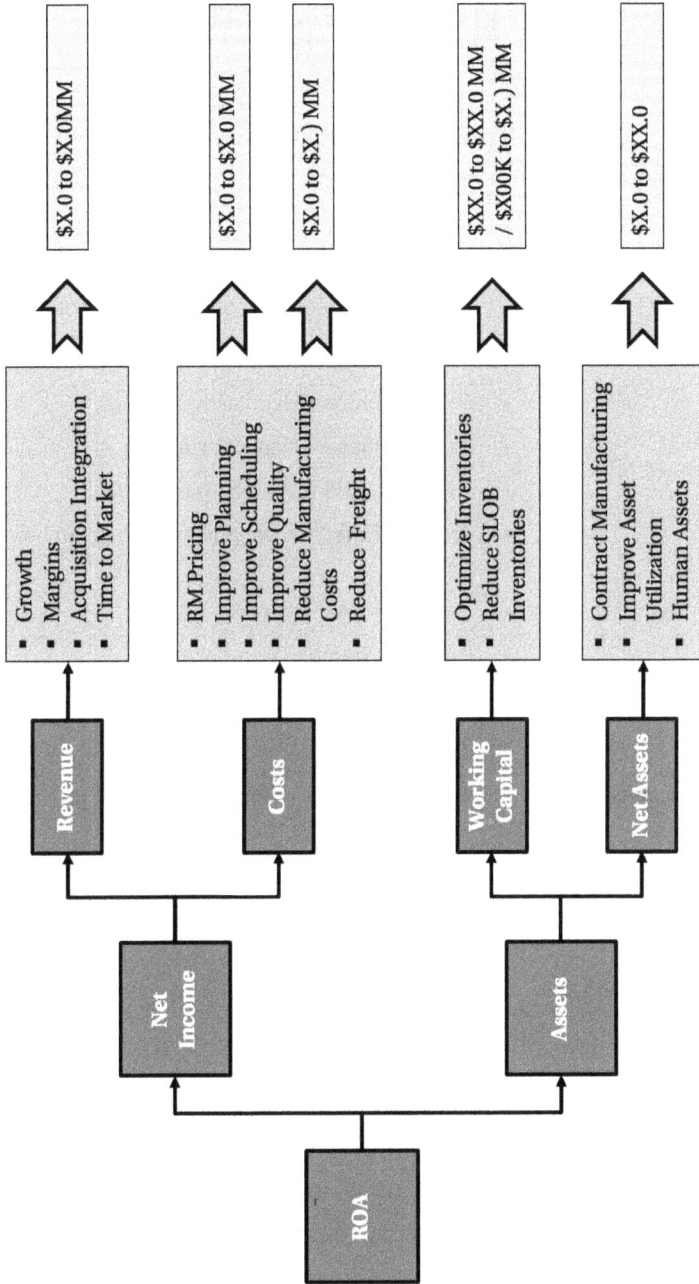

ROA → Net Income → Revenue →
- Growth
- Margins
- Acquisition Integration
- Time to Market

→ $X.0 to $X.0MM

Revenue → Costs →
- RM Pricing
- Improve Planning
- Improve Scheduling
- Improve Quality
- Reduce Manufacturing Costs
- Reduce Freight

→ $X.0 to $X.0 MM
→ $X.0 to $X.) MM

ROA → Assets → Working Capital →
- Optimize Inventories
- Reduce SLOB Inventories

→ $XX.0 to $XX.0 MM / $X00K to $X.) MM

Assets → Net Assets →
- Contract Manufacturing
- Improve Asset Utilization
- Human Assets

→ $X.0 to $XX.0

Example: Operating Costs

Optimized Operating Costs through better Planning of Assets

Interest Areas	• Improved scheduling to reduce overall manufacturing costs
	• Improved scheduling to reduce capacity constraints
	• Reduce overtime
	• Improve yields
	• Improve production reliability
	• Improve "First Time Quality" & Rework
	• Reduce energy costs
	• Reduce Contract Manufacturing needs
	• Improved Supply Network Planning
	• Improved WHS Inventory management
	• Reduced Expedited Freight and overall out bound logistic costs
	• Reduced warehouse costs
	• Balancing variable "Campaigns"
	• Improved WHS "Constraint Planning"
	• Integrate Logistic with Production
Examples	• Better Demand & Production Planning for $X.0 to $XX.0MM
Financial Target	• Cost reduction of 2% – 3% – $X.0 – $X.0MM
KPI's / Metrics	• Forecast Accuracy and Bias
	• Supply Plan Adherence

The business case for change is an invaluable tool to qualify and quantify what results are to be expected from the optimization or transformation project. You want to build out the business case for change with your project team(s). Be tough on the team to thoroughly vet the qualifying statements and quantifiable benefits. Specific examples are best to support your positions. If the project team believes you can increase revenue by 1-2%, give examples about how revenue may have been lost or what will increase it. If the project team believes you can reduce costs by 4-6%, give examples of how costs have been inflated or how waste has contributed to higher costs. Again, be specific and work to make your examples bulletproof. Most if not all, steering committees will want to see some form of a business case for change.

Performance Management System

A performance management system is used to ensure that performance goals are consistently being achieved and if not, it can identify why they are not. Performance management can focus on the performance of an organization, a department, employee, or even the processes to build a product or service, or products themselves.[29]

Armstrong and Baron (1998) defined it as a "strategic and integrated approach to increase the effectiveness of companies by improving the performance of the people who work in them and by developing the capabilities of teams and individual contributors."[30]

A performance management system is often used by the managers to align the goals of the company to the goals of their employees, thereby ensuring productivity.

I have been involved with performance management my entire career.

On the corporate side as an accountant, supply chain operations manager, sales manager, business director, general manager and vice president, performance management has always been a key management tool to guide, monitor and enhance performance.

In my consulting career, I am viewed as a performance management specialist working on a variety of projects where performance
management is a key element of the project.

What really surprises me is how organizations continue to struggle in
areas of performance management.

The Balanced Scorecard

I am a big fan of the balanced scorecard.

Various origins are identified as the originators of the balanced
scorecard including Art Schneiderman, Robert S Kaplan and David
P Norton. I was introduced to the balanced scorecard during my
graduate studies through the 1996 book by Kaplan and Norton, The
Balanced Scorecard.[31]

The balanced scorecard, at its roots, is a strategic planning and
performance management system.

The balanced scorecard was introduced in our MBA Program, as
our MBA was in strategic management. A strategic planning and
performance management system in a strategic management MBA
program looks perfectly aligned.

With my varied background in accounting, supply chain, operations
and sales and technology, the balanced scorecard made perfect
sense to me.

There have been various criticisms of the balanced scorecard and
a variety of variants of the balanced scorecard. To this day, I still
find it a valuable tool when developing a performance management system.

Kaplan and Norton found during their research in performance management that most organization's measurement systems were skewed toward financial measures. In their research, a "balanced" group of measures in the organization was not noted. Thus, the balanced scorecard tried to remedy this common approach to performance management.

The balanced scorecard focuses on "four perspectives" to identify strategic initiatives and KPIs to develop and track the implementation of your strategy.

KPIs are strategic measures that define the direction of the organization.

The Four Perspectives are:

- **Financial**: Identification of a few relevant high-level financial measures.
- **Customer**: Identification of measures that answer the question "What is important to our customers?"
- **Internal Business Processes**: Identification of measures that answer the question, "What must we excel at?"
- **Learning and Growth**: Identification of measures that answer the question "How can we continue to improve, create value and innovate?"[32]

When I was with Oracle, they had acquired new balanced scorecard software. The software was designed to help companies implement the BSC methodology.

I was on the sales and consulting side as a performance management SME.

I used a cool approach when preparing for a presentation and solution demonstration for a potential client.

I started by reviewing the client's annual report.

From the review of the annual report, I would identify the key strategic initiatives the company discussed in the annual report. I would then sort the initiatives into the four focus areas of the balanced scorecard.

From there, I would build a client-specific balanced scorecard model in the software aligning the financial, customer, internal business processes and learning and growth strategic initiatives.

I would next develop the KPIs for the initiatives to measure them.

I usually received interesting reactions to the presentation and software demonstration.

The first reaction would be very positive when the client could see their business with strategic initiatives and KPIs modeled in the software. I would walk them through how the software worked with their initiatives and KPIs right in front of them. Wow, they would be mesmerized.

I had a captivated audience.

Then at the end of the presentation and software demonstration, of course, I would ask if there were any questions.

Someone in the audience would inevitably make the following comment: "Jeez, we put too much of our strategy in our annual report. Our competitors know exactly what we are doing!"

Unfortunately, in a number of cases, the conversation would deteriorate rapidly into a discussion about the annual report.

As the Conductor of the presentation, I would have to bring the team back to the purpose of our meeting: how the Oracle-balanced scorecard software would enhance their balanced scorecard implementation.

As the pace of changes in business continues its rapid march forward, the number of strategic initiatives a company will be implementing will increase. Without a well-structured approach, it will be a challenge to management and their ability to deliver the benefits from the initiatives.

That is why I am still a strong proponent of the structure the balanced scorecard delivers.

Yes, there have been, and there will continue to be criticism of the balanced scorecard. What I have found is organizations and consultants try to make it too complicated. The discipline required to develop and maintain the complexity is what I consider a common failure mode.

My goal is to distill the complexity down to a manageable management system. The trick is how to apply The KISS System (Keep It Simple Stupid) to the complexity of business today.

What are your Strategic Initiatives?

- AI/ML
- Asset utilization
- Augmented reality (AR) or virtual reality (VR)
- Autonomous things
- Big Data
- Blockchain
- Cloud
- Customer strategy
- Cybersecurity
- Digitalization

- Future workforce
- In-memory computing
- Integrated business planning (IBP)/S&OP
- Internet of Things (IoT)
- Predictive and prescriptive analytics
- Product innovation
- Robotic process automation (RPA)
- Supply chain optimization, risk management chain optimization and risk management.

Once you have your strategic initiatives identified, what are the KPIs your organization will use for performance management?

A smart way to approach KPI development is to make them SMART!

KPIs should follow the SMART criteria:

- **S**pecific purpose for the business
- **M**easurable to really get value from the KPI
- **A**chievable or realistic
- **R**elevant to improving performance
- **T**ime-phased for a predefined and relevant period

Metrics are measures of quantitative assessment used for measurement, comparison or to track performance.[33]

Metrics are also performance indicators similar to KPIs.

The simplest way I differentiate between a KPI and metric is that KPIs are strategic and metrics are tactical. Some KPIs don't have any associated metrics. In many cases, a KPI is made up of multiple metrics.

Let's take a supply chain KPI, on-time and in-full, or OTIF. The KPI OTIF is a compound of two metrics, on-time and in-full. The on-time metric measures whether the delivery was made on time. If the delivery was scheduled for Wednesday at 2:00 p.m. and it did not happen until Thursday at 10:00 a.m., the delivery is not on time.

The in-full metric measures whether everything the customer ordered was delivered with the shipment. If the order was for 500 cases and only 450 cases were delivered, the order was not delivered in-full. Failure mode means either late delivery, short delivery, or both.

Companies measure OTIF on a monthly and yearly basis. OTIF can be sliced and diced across a variety of dimensions: geography, customer, warehouse and carrier.

The world is not short of KPIs and metrics. The challenge is having the right KPIs and metrics to manage your business and accurate data to support the KPIs and metrics.

Before I get into how I build out a performance management system, I would like to share a white paper called "The Illusion of Accuracy and Control."

The Illusion of Accuracy and Control

"I love this report! It is so detailed. We can make excellent business decisions with this level of detail!"

"I hate this report! It is so detailed; it is totally inaccurate. The quality of data at this granularity level is suspect, and we apply a number of allocations and average calculations to produce this report!"

These are comments from two employees at the same company, commenting on the same report. The first employee is the person who requested and created the report. The second employee is the business insights and analytics representative who developed the technology required to produce the report.

How can two people have such diametrically opposed opinions of the same report? It is a perception called "The Illusion of Accuracy."

Merriam-Webster defines Illusion as:

- The action of deceiving
- The state or act of being intellectually deceived or misled
- An instance of deception
- A misleading image presented to the vision
- Something that deceives or misleads intellectually
- A perception of something objectively existing in such a way as to cause the misinterpretation of its actual nature[34]

"The Illusion of Accuracy" is more common than most would think when evaluating enterprise-level business insights and analytics reporting systems (i.e., the consultant's new name for a performance management system).

The illusion stems from the deceptions of information accuracy and the ill-advised innate feeling of control. Thus, the name of this white paper, "The Illusion of Accuracy and Control."

Let me set the stage for the initial development of the illusion of accuracy and control.

I will start off by saying the phrase is not of my creation.

A young member of the information technology staff on the project of origin was the person who coined the phrase.

He was a perceptive young man, able to articulate what we were all sensing and struggling to describe into this, simple singular phrase: "The Illusion of Accuracy."

The client had hired us to evaluate their Enterprise performance management system relating to KPI quality, and dashboard and reports along with the technical architecture that supports the performance management system.

As part of the forensic analysis of KPIs (Archaeologists), we use a document called an "Operational Definition" of each KPI. The "Operational Definition" includes information concerning the corporate strategy (safety, performance, innovations, customers); KPI governance (who owns the KPI); KPI data sources /integrity/dimensions and KPI calculations along with the frequency of reporting.

The KPI that supports the aforementioned report was quite complicated.

It was measuring the performance of a particular cost element in manufacturing operations allocating costs across product lines and products.

As we dove deeper into the calculations, it became apparent that there were many subjective allocations and a variety of composite averages (average of an average distorts the accuracy of the KPI).

Additionally, the data coming from multiple sources was suspect.

Generating the report on a monthly basis took a number of hours to run as it spanned a global set of manufacturing plants.

When all was said and done, this monster of a KPI report produced information at a very low level of granularity.

This is now where "the illusion of accuracy" manifests itself.

If the report is that detailed with this level of granularity, the information must be correct and accurate.

As Agatha Christie's quirky Belgian detective Hercule Poirot would articulate, "Au contraire, mon ami! It is the absolute opposite!"

The report is the most inaccurate representation of reality! Suspect source data, allocations, averages upon averages totally distort the accuracy of the information.

Thus, "the illusion of accuracy!"

The more detailed and granular, the more accurate the information should be. Right? Wrong!

This KPI and report were the tip of the proverbial iceberg.

We prepped the CIO, one of our sponsors, on our findings before the next project review to give him a heads up.

He immediately displayed the first two stages of the five stages of grief: denial and anger. To him, we were: "wrong," or "stupid."

Over the next couple of days, the CIO advanced through bargaining, depression and finally hit acceptance.

It was a good thing we got him to acceptance before the project review meeting with the CFO and various sponsors from the business.

During the project review, we walked the client team through our overall finding. We had prepared one slide for "the illusion of accuracy."

As we presented "the illusion of accuracy," the CFO, normally a very cool customer, leaned forward with his elbows on the conference room table, and a frown on his face. He stated with a tone of obvious irritation in his voice, "You have got to be kidding me."

Was this a question or a statement of fact?

He then turned to the CIO and asked if our findings about the accuracy of KPIs were true. The CIO responded, "Yes." There was no need to go further as you can imagine the next part of the conversation.

By the way, we gave full credit to the young gentleman from the information technology team for coining the phrase and shedding light on the issue.

If we go back to the Merriam-Webster definition of Illusion, you can understand the emotional element of being deceived where the truth is the opposite of what you are being told.

- The action of deceiving
- The state or act of being intellectually deceived or misled
- The instance of deception
- A misleading image presented to the vision
- Something that deceives or misleads intellectually
- A perception of something objectively existing in such a way as to cause misinterpretation of its actual nature

Fast forward a few years to another client where we will blend "the illusion of accuracy" with "the illusion of control" to bring it all together to create: "the illusion of accuracy and control."

Before we get to "the illusion of control," let me say that I have used "the illusion of accuracy" conversation on a number of projects with a number of clients in the time period between "the illusion of accuracy" and "the illusion of control." It is always an interesting, and sometimes emotionally charged, conversation with clients when they grasp their own reality as to the illusion of accuracy.

It is always an interesting conversation when I identify a reporting system that "distorts reality." Half the time, employees use the recommend reports but have NO idea how the KPI is calculated.

When you review the calculation, it is in many cases like pulling teeth to find the owner of the KPI and calculation.

Many "aha" moments have been encountered when diving into the guts of the KPIs.

Did I mention I love the Archaeologist work? We are starting to solve mysteries here!

"The illusion of control" comes from a project where I was tasked with transforming a significant business practice.

Like all processes that are not controlled by a continuous improvement plan, the business processes of this business practice had morphed into a very complex, multifaceted collection of inputs and outputs driven from a sophisticated information technology platform.

The initial phase of the project called for the client to walk us through their existing business processes.

We sat in on workshops where the client teams documented their current "as-is" business processes.

Wow, there were so many sub-processes and lines connecting processes to the information technology platform that the work almost brought Visio to its knees. That takes a lot to get them there!

The client had never documented their business processes like this before, so as we progressed through the workshops, you could see them realizing that they had created unsustainable processes and a complexity that few understood.

This same story is told over and over again with different clients on different projects.

After we finished documenting the "as-is" business processes, we turned our attention to the performance management system the client had developed to control and monitor the various aspects of the business processes.

Wow, again.

The reports were so complex and overly detailed.

We were not exactly sure what they were trying to represent in the report.

It was information and data overload for sure.

When asked a simple question about the content of a report, we would be taken on a 30-minute dissertation explaining what was in the report and how it was used by the business.

You needed a legend to understand what the report was showing and how to interpret the information.

Complex business processes and complex reporting triggered my thoughts of "the illusion of accuracy."

We like to have honest discussions with clients. We work hard to build trust and commit ourselves to look out for their best interests. We're not pointing fingers or criticizing. But sometimes the questions can make people uncomfortable, in particular when it is their area of responsibility.

I reviewed the origins of "the illusion of accuracy," explaining the context of the project and the problems. We gave credit to the sharp young technologist who had coined the phrase. We were getting a lot of head nodding and head shaking as we reviewed how "the illusion of accuracy" was affecting their organization.

At the end of the afternoon session, the client project leader made the proverbial leap. "We not only have an illusion of accuracy; we also have the illusion of control!"

He went on to explain the organizational cultural (Anthropologist) aspect of "illusion of control." "There is a perception, right or wrong, that the more details provided in reports, the more control managers have over business activities. The reality is that they have less control."

The project leader went on to further explain, "There is a cultural norm to get buried in the details, but as we do, we lose track of the 'Big Picture.' We are always in the weeds! Short-term decisions to move the needle an inch vs. long-term decisions to move the needle to the max. On the other hand, many manage by gut feel vs. data. Which makes sense because who can understand what our data is showing because it is so detailed and complex. Gut feel is the way they make decisions. We have an 'illusion of control' along with an 'illusion of accuracy.'"

So now we have linked "accuracy" with "control" to formulate "the illusion of accuracy and control." Because of the "inaccuracy" of information, we actually have less "control" over processes and business decisions.

During the next project steering committee meeting, we presented a slide titled "the illusion of accuracy and control."

The client project leader had documented three examples of "the illusion of accuracy and control for presentation to the steering committee.

He was able to quickly rattle off details of each example to provide the color commentary.

When he asked if there were any questions, no one spoke. After another pause of silence, only a comment from a senior leader on the steering committee popped up, "We've got a lot of work ahead of us to change these cultural norms."

So, now you've seen how I developed the phrase, "the illusion of accuracy and control."

And I hopefully shared two interesting stories about the origins of the phrase. But you might be thinking to yourself, *so what*? That question is totally understandable. Let's discuss now what it means in today's world.

Conclusion

- The illusion of accuracy and control is alive and well in corporations around the world.
- Where does your organization rate when it comes to the illusion of accuracy and control?
- Where does your organization rate when it comes to data governance?
- Where does your organization rate when it comes to business insights and analytics governance?
- What are your strategies and plans for "Big Data"?
- There are a lot of questions to be answered, along with a lot of concerns to be addressed!

Building a Strategic Initiative and KPI Matrix

There is a lot of discussion around companies having too many strategic initiatives and KPIs. Well, if you look at the list of the strategic initiatives companies are working on today, there is a lot going on.

For a while, I was in that camp. But my thought processes have now evolved.

My background is mostly in manufacturing and distribution.

The American Production and Inventory Control Society (APICS)[35], has a Supply Chain Operations Reference (SCOR) model, which I use extensively.

The basic SCOR model categorizes the supply chain business processes as plan, source, make, deliver and return.

I personally like what some call the Extended SCOR model of innovate, sell, plan, source, make, deliver, service and return. This brings R&D, sales, marketing and a service organization into a more integrated business flow.

The illustration on page 220 identifies the integrated business processes across the Extended SCOR Model.

Under the processes is a bar labeled strategic initiatives.

Below are some of the strategic initiatives divvied up by process area.

In the lower section of the chart are the four elements of the balanced scorecard.

This is to represent that the financial customer, internal business processes and learning and innovation cut across all of the Extended SCOR activities. Meaning, an organization should have strategic initiatives and KPIs for financial, customer, internal business processes and learning and innovation aligned with these steps: innovate, sell, plan, source, make, deliver, service and return.

At the bottom of the illustration, is a bar that calls out the impact of information technology across the Extended SCOR Model.

If your organization is not in manufacturing and distribution, but you specialize in insurance, financial services, healthcare, build the linear models of your major business processes and align with the Balanced Scorecard categories.

The visual on page 221 is the matrix where you populate the strategic initiatives in the individual boxes. What this does is show gaps where your existing strategic initiatives may not be hitting all of the balanced scorecard buckets. The work I do with clients is to make sure we have strategic initiatives that will drive performance across the Extended SCOR model aligned with financial, customer, internal business processes and learning and innovation.

This is a very powerful way of looking at your strategic initiatives to identify significant gaps.

The beauty of the matrix is in its power, flexibility and adaptability.

The matrix will produce 32 strategic initiatives boxes. I will say that not every box has to be populated with a strategic initiative because not every company has this much going on.

Some companies may have more than one strategic initiative in a box. Maybe there is more than one strategic initiative at the intersection of "make and internal processes."

Business Strategies for KPI Development

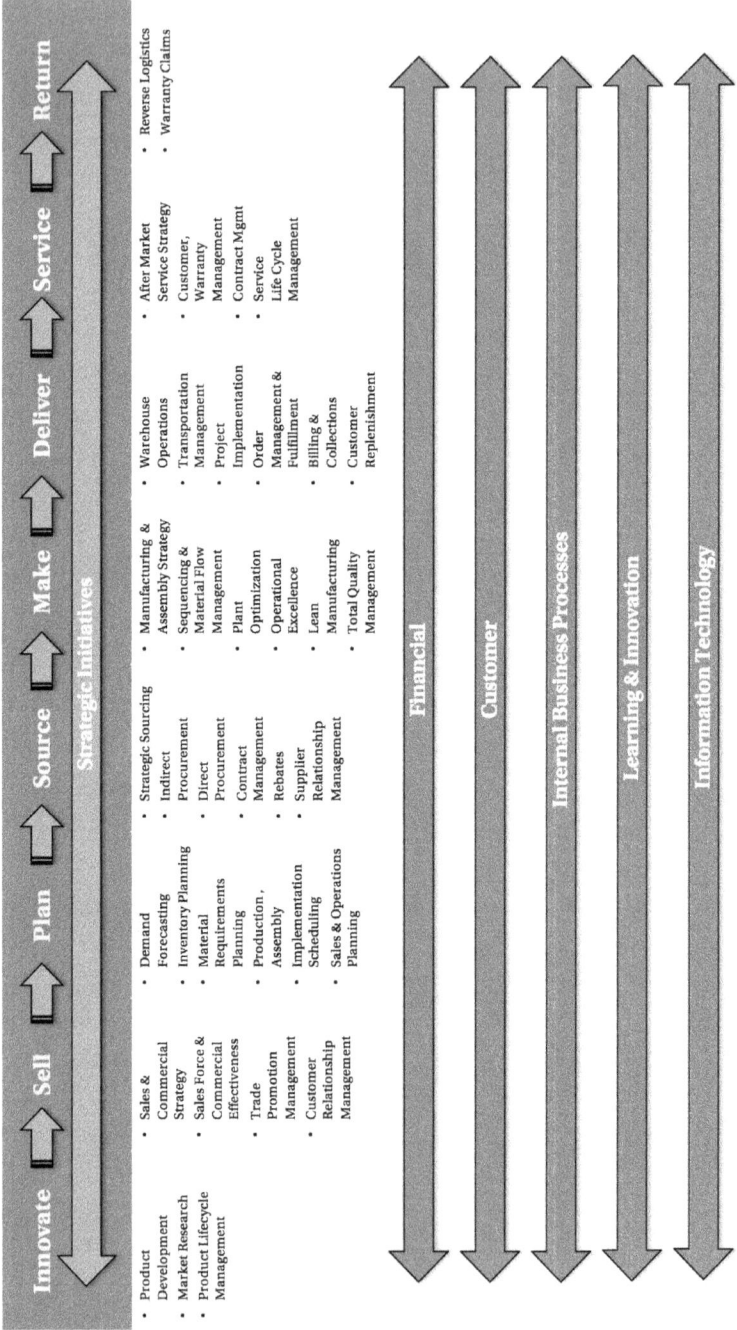

Strategic Initiatives

Innovate	Sell	Plan	Source	Make	Deliver	Service	Return
• Product Development • Market Research • Product Lifecycle Management	• Sales & Commercial Strategy • Sales Force & Commercial Effectiveness • Trade Promotion Management • Customer Relationship Management	• Demand Forecasting • Inventory Planning • Material Requirements Planning • Production, Assembly • Implementation Scheduling • Sales & Operations Planning	• Strategic Sourcing • Indirect Procurement • Direct Procurement • Contract Management • Rebates • Supplier Relationship Management	• Manufacturing & Assembly Strategy • Sequencing & Material Flow Management • Plant Optimization • Operational Excellence • Lean Manufacturing • Total Quality Management	• Warehouse Operations • Transportation Management • Project Implementation • Order Management & Fulfillment • Billing & Collections • Customer Replenishment	• After Market Service Strategy • Customer, Warranty Management • Contract Mgmt • Service Life Cycle Management	• Reverse Logistics • Warranty Claims

Financial

Customer

Internal Business Processes

Learning & Innovation

Information Technology

Strategic Initiatives Distribution

	Financial	Customer	Internal Process	Learning & Innovation
Innovate				
Sell				
Plan				
Source				
Make				
Deliver				
Service				
Return				

	Financial	Customer	Internal Process	Learning & Innovation
Innovate	R&D Agility		R&D Agility	S&OP
Sell		Integrated Globalization		S&OP
Plan	Supply Chain Savings	Integrated Globalization	Supply Chain Savings	S&OP
Source	Supply Chain Savings	Integrated Globalization	Supply Chain Savings	S&OP
Make	Supply Chain Savings	Integrated Globalization	Supply Chain Savings	S&OP
Deliver	Supply Chain Savings	Integrated Globalization	Supply Chain Savings	S&OP
Service				
Return	Supply Chain Savings		Supply Chain Savings	

The point is this matrix can help guide a company to evaluate what buckets the strategic initiatives are hitting and where there may be gaps.

The next tool on page 223 is the matrix and the populated KPIs to support the Initiatives. This depiction shows gaps where existing KPIs may not be hitting all of the balanced scorecard buckets. The work I do with clients, ensures we have KPIs that will drive performance across the strategic initiatives in the Extended SCOR model aligned with financial, customer, internal business processes and learning and innovation, balanced scorecard categories.

This is a very powerful way of looking at your KPIs to identify significant gaps and there are usually a number of them.

The next resource on page 224 is the matrix and populated metrics to support the KPIs.

Note: Not all KPIs will have underlying metrics. The KPI and metric may be the same.

The flow from strategic initiative to KPI to metric is called cascading. The three matrices cascade from strategy to KPI to metric. The three matrices cascade across these steps: innovate, sell, plan, source, make deliver, service and return.

Companies can use this as part of their performance review and compensation system to cascade down through the levels of the organization.

Note: Some companies will want to break out and innovate into R&D and marketing or sell into marketing and sales. This may work better for some companies where those functions are truly viewed separately.

KPI Distribution

	Financial	Customer	Internal Process	Learning & Innovation
Innovate				
Sell				
Plan				
Source				
Make				
Deliver				
Service				
Return				

	Financial	Customer	Internal Process	Learning & Innovation
Innovate			New Product Time to Market	
Sell		Global Market Penetration		
Plan	Working Capital			Forecast & BIAS Accuracy
Source	Raw Material Costs		Supplier Scorecards	
Make	Manufacturing Costs		Manufacturing Efficiencies	Manufacturing Efficiencies
Deliver	Logistic Costs	On Time in Full (OTIF)		
Service		Customer Scorecards		
Return	Logistic Costs		RMA Process	

Metric Distribution

	Financial	Customer	Internal Process	Learning & Innovation
Innovate				
Sell				
Plan				
Source				
Make				
Deliver				
Service				
Return				

	Financial	Customer	Internal Process	Learning & Innovation
Innovate	R&D Costs % of Sales			
Sell		India % Increase		Forecast & BIAS Accuracy
Plan	Inventory Turns			Forecast & BIAS Accuracy
Source	Additive Savings		Quality Rating	
Make	Waste $		Supply Plan Adherence	Contract Manufacturing Optimization
Deliver	Expedited Freight	On Time in Full (OTIF)		
Service		Customer Satisfaction		
Return	Railcar Utilization			

KPI Governance and Operational Definitions

Another important area for business insights and analytics is the governance of KPIs, metrics and reports.

KPIs, metrics and reports should be governed by a cross-functional team for the holistic management of the KPI, metrics and reports.

The KPI governance team has the responsibility to ensure that KPIs, metrics and reports accurately reflect the information being presented.

The KPI, metrics and report owners, definition, calculations and the data sources must be clearly identified and documented.

I use an operational definition form, which defines all the parameters associated with the KPI, metrics and reports.

In our example, we are going to use an operational definition to specify the properties of a KPI or metrics.

On the first project highlighted in the illusion of accuracy and control, the client hired us to review their KPIs and metrics. When we started the project, we asked them for some form of a document that defined the properties of their KPIs and metrics. This will be a foreign concept to many companies as it was with one particular client.

There was no documentation, showing us some of the issues we were brought in to fix.

Building an operational definition requires a good amount of infor-mation for clarity and transparency. In the operational definition we use, there are 33 data elements to complete the operational definition.

Operational Definition Master Data

- Metric name
- Metric #
- Corporate strategy supported
- Function
- Stakeholder/owner
- Metric steward
- Subjects area
- Metric definition
- Metric effect on RONA
- Data source(s)
- Data source(s) ID
- Statistical or non-statistical
- Discrete or continuous
- Unit of measure
- Calculations
- Aggregation rules
- Time period

Dimension

- Business
- Segment
- Business Entity
- SBU
- Market segment
- Customer

Product (Asset)

- Product family

- Product line
- Sub-product line
- Grade
- Item

Geography

- Region of sale
- Region of manufacturing
- RB performance units
- Entity
- Location

An example of part of the operation definition form for days sales outstanding (DSO) can be found on page 228. Days sales outstanding is an important KPI when managing working capital.

The highest level KPI for this client was return on net assets (RONA). All the KPIs and metrics were judged against their effect on RONA.

When we started the project, none of this was documented. So, it took some time to pull this level of detail together, as we were performing our functions as an archaeologist building artifacts. We also obtained a view into their culture, helping us understand our work as the Anthropologist.

Once we had done this, the fun started.

This chart uses a similar concept as the work of color-coding the process boxes on the process flow maps and looking for root causes of the problems in the performance management system.

Operational Definition: DSO

Operational Definition - DSO

Define *What* you are trying to Measure

Field	Value	Description
Metric Name	DSO	Corporation Metric Name
Metric #	Fin01	Control Number
Corporate Strategy Supported	Performance	Safety, Performance, Innovations, Customers (Levers - Margin Improvement, Capacity & Emerging Market Expansion, Porfolio Management, New Product Development)
Function	Sales	Finance, Supply Chain, Operations, Sales, Feed Stock, Purchasing, MfG, Treasury, Tax, Cont's GRP
Stakeholder / Owner	VP Sales	VP Sales, VP Manufacturing, Controller, Plant Manager
Metric Steward	Finance	Finance, Supply Chain, Operations, Sales, Feed Stock, Purchasing, MfG, Treasury, Tax, Cont's GRP - In charge of reporting, maintains integrity of Metric.
Subjects Area	Net Working Capital	Variable Margin, Fixed Manufacturing Costs, STA, Net Working Capital, PP&E
Metric Definition	Days Sales Outstanding (DSO) figure is an index of the relationship between outstanding receivables and credit account sales achieved over a given period. The DSO analysis provides general information about the number of days on average that customers take to pay invoices.	Understandable Description of the Metric

Decide *How* you will attach a value to the Metric (Does it effect RONA +/-)

Field	Value	Description
Metric Effect on RONA	An increase in DSO can result in cash flow problems and have a negative effect on RONA. A decrease in DSO can result in cash flow improvements and have a positive effect on RONA.	Describe the conditions of how the metric effects RONA

Decide *How* you will collect the data for the Metric (Data Source(s), Statistical or Non Statistical Control, Discrete or Continuous Data)

Field	Value	Description
Data Source(s)	JDE	Describe the Data Source such as JDE, Manufacturing Systems, Quality Systems, CRM, 3rd Party Data, Excel Spreadsheet
Data Source(s) ID	DS1234	Data Source ID Number
Statistical or Non Statistical	Non Statistical	Statistical Control would be a metric generated from Data Source where Control Charts are used to capture statistical accurate data
Discrete or Continuous	Continuous	Discrete Data is based on Yes/No, Open/Closed, Male/Female type data. Continuous Data is data monitored over time.

Decide *How* you will record the data for the Metric (Unit of Measure, Calculations, Aggregation Rules)

Field	Value	Description
Unit of Measure	Days	What is the unit of measure: $, €, lbs., gallons, %
Calculations	DSO = (Receivables/Sales) * Days in Period	Detailed description of how the metric is calculated

As we walked through each one of the KPIs/metrics and reviewed the data elements, there were a lot of surprises. And more than a fair share of finger-pointing.

"What do you mean there needs to be an owner and steward of the KPI?"

"These can't be the data sources for that KPI. That makes no sense."

"I didn't know that was how the KPI was calculated. That explains everything."

"Why is that allocated to that business? They have nothing to do with this KPI."

"No wonder that product line is always losing money."

"No one uses that metric. It's a piece of crap."

Point here being; if you don't have operational definitions for your KPIs and metrics, I would highly suggest you get started. This will be a good basis for identifying root cause issues in your performance management system.

Business Insights and Analytics

Now that an organization has its strategic initiatives, KPIs and metrics nailed down; it's time to use analytics to manage all this information. I'll start with a few definitions and then discuss what some of the major players are doing with analytics.

Industry Definitions

Institute for Advanced Analytics

Advanced analytics is a part of data science that uses high-level methods and tools to focus on projecting future trends, events and behaviors. This gives organizations the ability to perform advanced statistical models such as "what-if" calculations, as well as to future-proof various aspects of their operations.

This term is an umbrella for several sub-fields of analytics that work together in their predictive capabilities.

The major areas that make up advanced analytics are predictive data analytics, big data and data mining.

Gartner

Gartner describes advanced analytics as the autonomous or semi-autonomous examination of data or content using sophisticated techniques and tools, typically beyond those of traditional business intelligence (BI), to discover deeper insights, make predictions, or generate recommendations. Advanced analytic techniques include data/text mining, ML, pattern matching, forecasting, visualization, semantic analysis, sentiment analysis, network and cluster analysis, multivariate statistics, graph analysis, simulation, complex event processing, neural networks.[35]

Descriptive, Predictive, Prescriptive Analytics

There are three types of analytics used as common reference points: descriptive, predictive and prescriptive. The following are definitions for Descriptive, Predictive and Prescriptive Analytics:

Descriptive

The first stage of business analytics is Descriptive Analytics, which still account for the majority of all business analytics today.

Descriptive Analytics look at past performance and understand that performance by mining historical data to look for the reasons behind past success or failure.

Descriptive Analytics are the examination of data or content, usually manually performed, to answer the question "What happened?" (or "What is happening?"), characterized by traditional business intelligence (BI) and visualizations such as pie charts, bar charts, line graphs, tables or generated narratives.[36]

Predictive

Predictive Analytics encompass a variety of statistical techniques, from data mining, predictive modeling and machine learning, that analyze current and historical facts to make predictions about future or otherwise unknown events.[37]

In business, predictive models exploit patterns found in historical and transactional data to identify risks and opportunities. Models capture relationships among many factors to allow assessment of risk or potential associated with a particular set of conditions, guiding decision-making for candidate transactions.

Predictive Analytics answer the question of what is likely to happen. This is when historical data is combined with rules, algorithms and occasionally external data to determine the probable future outcome of an event or the likelihood of a situation occurring.

Prescriptive[38]

Prescriptive Analytics are the third and final phase of business analytics, which also includes Descriptive and Predictive Analytics.

Prescriptive Analytics go beyond predicting future outcomes by also suggesting actions to benefit from the predictions and showing the implications of each decision option.

Referred to as the "final frontier of analytic capabilities," Prescriptive Analytics entail the application of mathematical and computational sciences, and suggest decision options to take advantage of the results of Descriptive and Predictive Analytics.

SAP

SAP data analytics solutions allow organizations to make intelligent business connections. Using new data sources and being able to determine what is valuable and what is noise is no easy feat. Without the time or means to evolve — or technology that's flexible enough to grow with your business — you can only achieve the status quo. Innovation will have to wait.[39]

Microsoft

Traditional BI tools, such as Tableau, Qlik, etc., are solutions for analysts that provide rearview mirror intelligence on what has happened. In contrast, Power BI is a business analytics service that can empower everyone — not just data specialists — with real-time insight into what is happening. With Power BI, it takes five minutes to start creating personalized dashboards to find answers to the most important questions for your business.[40]

Tableau

When it comes to elevating people with the power of data, only Tableau combines a laser focus on how people see and understand data with the kind of robust, scalable platform you need to run even the world's largest organizations. The Tableau platform turns data into insights that drive action.[41]

Business Insights and Analytics Data Governance

The root cause of the "illusion of accuracy" concerns the lack of governance around data, KPIs and reports. Many organizations still need to "get their house in order" concerning the cleanliness and accuracy of their data.

Master data and operational data management are insufficiently managed in many organizations. Data stewards who develop data strategies and work on continuous improvement of data quality are critical in today's data-driven world.

Implementing a methodology such as Six Sigma to manage master and operational data can be a viable platform to improve the quality of data.

In the chart below, you will see the different levels of Six Sigma data accuracy. If an organization has a rating of 3.5, they are in the "Good" category. If they are below 3.5, they need to improve their rating. If they are above 3.5, the organization is doing very well. A simple test would be to take a sample of 1,000 data elements and determine the organization's Sigma level. You'll know pretty quickly whether the organization has some work on their hands. DPMO stands for

Defects Per Million Opportunities; it measures the number of identified defects per a 1 million sample size.

Six Sigma Rating

	Six Sigma Level	% Accuracy	DPMO
Virtually Perfect	6	99.9997%	3.43.4
Excellent	5	99.98%	233
Very Good	4	99.4%	6,210
Good	3.5	97.7%	22,700
Needs Some Improvement	3	93.3%	66,807
Needs Much Improvement	2	69.1%	308,537

Data Integration / Master Data Management (MDM) Technology

Informatica[42] and Alteryx[43] are two of the leading data integration/ MDM technology providers and their solutions. These technology providers create solutions in MDM and ETL (extract, transform and load). These solutions help you manage and cleanse your data.

Big Data

We hear about "Big Data this and Big Data that." If you don't have your master and operational data under control, you should have serious reservations about jumping too far into "Big Data." Big Data

= Big Problems if you don't have your data management and governance processes under control.

Summary

I hope the discussion in this area has been insightful for you. As you can see, I have done a significant body of work in performance management and have developed useful and practical approaches. These useful and practical approaches can help you, too.

I still find The Balanced Scorecard a powerful methodology to develop strategic initiatives, KPIs and metrics. When you combine it with the Extended SCOR model, the power is magnified multi-fold.

Companies and people need structure when developing strategic initiatives, KPIs and metrics. These two methodologies provide a very visual approach to validating your work.

If the Extended SCOR model does not fit your industry, develop a model that does.

Make sure you document your KPIs and metrics with operational definitions. You'll learn a lot about your organization and uncover a lot of issues that can be developed into continuous improvement projects.

As we discussed in the last section on master data, operational data needs close attention. You have to get your house in order, or your organization will be wasting time and money chasing its tail.

Here's another takeaway for this chapter: improve is the fourth stage of Six Sigma. Whether you implement Six Sigma or not, improve is very important for long-term data sustainability.

And finally, the world of advanced analytics is right at our feet. Tremendous technical progress has been made in recent years. A variety of solution providers are available to help any organization.

CHAPTER 7
POLICIES

A policy, either written or unwritten, is a principle to guide decisions through logical or controlled outcomes. A policy is a "statement of intent."[44]

A written policy, as in an accounting policy, is very specific as to the expected process and outcome.

An unwritten policy is a cultural norm through either institutional or tribal knowledge, which guides the organization or specific group in making decisions or affecting behavior.

In consulting, our tribal policy is to arrive at the client's early before the majority of employees and not to depart until a majority of employees have left for the day. If we can arrive before the leadership team and depart after the leadership team, that is even better.

You can find written and unwritten policies in R&D, marketing, sales, supply chain, operations, HR, finance and accounting and information technology.

Policies can be found at an office, a plant, or in a country, region, or anywhere in the world.

There are way too many policy examples to discuss in this book.

So, let's focus on how policies affect optimization and transformation projects.

Information Technology Policies

Software systems have built-in policies that guide their operation. These policies come in the form of settings. Each setting will guide the software to perform in a particular way, which comprises the policies the software provider has built into its software.

The software is making decisions based on the settings. The software provider will, in many cases, supply standard settings because they have found that these settings optimize the performance of the software. This is why they highly recommend that you don't change those settings.

If you hire a consulting company to help with the software implementation, they will have their own policies on the settings which may be aligned with the software provider or which may be different. In many cases, the consultant will apply their preferred settings, which will modify the way the software makes decisions and performs and the consultant has now modified the policies of the software provider in the application. This can be good or bad. It depends on how the system operates to meet your need.

Note: I have seen specific cases where even the software provider's own consultants change the settings.

With any software implementation, it is critical that your team totally understand the settings and how they affect policy decisions being made by the software. They need to understand the cause and effect of the setting in a standard or modified form.

I was hired by a technology and consulting company as vice president of services to transform their implementation methodology. One of my first tasks was for the teams to walk me through the software.

I started with our North American implementation teams. As we were going through the demonstration and hit a particular process, one of the consultants asked the presenter why the software was transacting in a certain way. The presenter said, "That's the way it always performs for this transaction." The consultant who posed the question replied, "That is not how I have seen that transaction processed on my implementations."

We got into a very fruitful discussion and found that there were competing ideas on the settings for the transaction that affected how the transaction was handled as well as the policies of the software. So, I had conflicting implementation settings for this transaction from two North American team members.

Two weeks later, I headed off to meet with our European consulting team. We went through the same software demonstration. When we hit that particular transaction, I saw a different setting and the way the transaction was processed. I mentioned to the team that I had seen three different settings in the way the transaction was processed. I asked if this was client-specific or region-specific and they said no.

Now I had at least three settings for the same transaction and three policies. Software follows process flows, which means this transaction moving downstream in the flow of software; may produce three different outcomes and effect multiple policies of the software.

I could see we had a lot of work to do with our implementation methodology.

In another example, I was helping a client with inventories. The project focused on inventory governance, inventory optimization, inventory rationalization and inventory disposition.

When we began the inventory optimization analysis, I reviewed their demand and inventory planning system. It was a pretty good system that very well met their needs.

There are a few critical settings in the planning system concerning customer service levels, safety stock and lead times. These settings govern the inventory policies that are built into the software. What I found was that the client had some inventory governance policies that had not yet come to light.

"The policy" was that the company would "never miss a shipment because they were out of stock/inventory." This was pretty aggressive across all SKUs, never to be out of stock on any SKU.

A leading practice is to assign different customer service levels to A, B, C and D SKUs. If you are not familiar with A, B, C, D classification, A refers to your fast movers who drive a significant portion of your Sales. A SKUs can follow the 80/20 Rule meaning 80% of sales would come from the A SKUs, and 20% of sales would come from the B, C and D SKUs.

Note: The ironic part is that planners usually spend 80% of their time on the B, C and D SKUs and 20% of their time on the A SKUs! But that's a discussion for a different time.

The client had assigned a 99.9% customer service level to all their SKUs. The leading practice for non-life-threatening A SKUs is 98.5%. This means that there is a 1.5% "possibility" that you will have a stock out on this SKU. The difference between a 98.5% customer service level and 99.9% is NOT LINEAR; it is EXPONENTIAL. The client had implemented an inventory policy that effected the settings, which drove a significant increase in inventories to meet the almost 100% guarantee not to be Out of Stock.

The client did not trust the safety stock calculations the system recommended. The safety stock calculation is driven from settings and is governed by system policies. The client decided to pad the safety stock inventory in excess of the system recommended level. This was yet another unwritten policy.

The client was importing a significant number of SKUs. Because of some of their planning and purchasing approaches, their actual lead times were say 85 days. In the planning system, they padded the lead times to 105 days across all the SKUs. This policy and setting again drove to excess inventories.

The results of these inventory policies and system settings were that the planning system policies governing inventory drove a significant amount of excess inventory. Excess inventory equals slow-moving inventory, and low inventory turns and tied up working capital.

Overly conservative policies for customer service levels, safety stock and lead times resulted in inflated settings, which drove the planning systems' inventory policies to pad inventories.

Based on machine learning comparing demand to inventory levels, the system was actually telling them that they had too much inventory.

Our recommendation was for them to start to build confidence by modeling the new customer service levels, safety stock and lead times setting in a test system to determine the impact on inventory levels.

Institutional and Tribal Knowledge Policies

The consultants and your corporate team have the software "configured," meaning the settings have been established, and it's time to demonstrate the software to the users. If the software is replacement software, say a new financial system, the users will have had policies that govern transactions in the old system. Although they are both financial systems, the software can transact differently.

One of the hardest issues that users have to overcome is how the new system operates vs. the old system and how the transactions that govern the system's policies behave.

There can be institutional and tribal knowledge policies among the financial system users for how certain transactions are handled in the old system. These, in many cases, are workarounds people have developed over the years.

System policies and institutional and tribal knowledge policies all have to be relearned.

In our next example, let's look at the implementation of a new production planning system software in an organization.

Currently, production planning is done in Excel. There could be institutional and tribal knowledge policies among the production planners on the policies they use for production planning. More often than not, if you have multiple manufacturing plants, the production planner(s) at each plant will have their own institutional and tribal policies.

The new production planning system will come with its own policies on how to govern planning. The consultant and corporate team need to understand the localized institutional and tribal policies for production planning. This is very important from a change management and training standpoint. The production planners at the plants may have 15 years of experience in planning in Excel, and now the new planning system policies will be totally different.

I use these technology examples as an attempt to show that there are policies all over the organization and that they are written and unwritten. When people think of policies, we need to include more than the traditional ones that immediately come to mind.

Process Transformation Policies

Let's take my favorite project, "Mega Mystery," as an example of business process transformation policies.

- Level 0 is the business practice.
- Level 1, 3, are the business processes.
- Level 2, 21, are the business processes.
- Level 3 includes multiple business processes under each Level 2 process.

Each one of these processes is governed by written and/or unwritten policies.

If you remember, as we were reviewing the level 3 processes and color-coding them red, yellow and green, we used the 5 Whys for asking questions about why a process was red, yellow and green.

What we identified were some written, but mostly unwritten institutional, and tribal knowledge policies that governed how a process was handled, and decisions were made.

It was the identification of these policies that, in many cases, drove a process to red or yellow.

Most of these policies were related to symptoms.

Most policies that govern how business is transacted and how decisions are made are not documented. They are institutional and tribal knowledge policies.

When decomposing the business processes with the 5 Whys, the policies that come from the discussions provide valuable insights into cultural norms and are part of the artifacts you are documenting.

Whether you are in the corporate office or on the manufacturing shop floor, it is the unwritten institutional, and tribal knowledge policies that govern how processes are executed and decisions are made.

When undertaking a business or process transformation project, it is the understanding of the written and unwritten institutional and tribal knowledge policies that will lead you through the root cause analysis as you uncover what the true root cause(s) is.

In my favorite project, it was understanding the impact of the written and unwritten institutional and tribal knowledge policies that brought us to the root cause.

Summary

In both information technology and business processes, there are a massive amount of written and unwritten institutional and tribal knowledge policies.

Good luck in trying to document all of them.

When it comes to information technology system settings and policies; it is important for your team to understand the standard settings and policies of software and how they affect upstream and downstream processes and system decisions.

Before making changes to the standard settings and policies, understand the impact any changes will make in how the system will make decisions.

During the root cause analysis around optimization and transformation, capturing written and unwritten institutional and tribal knowledge policies will provide the artifact, clues and cultural norms of the organization.

CHAPTER 8

ORGANIZATIONAL CHANGE MANAGEMENT

I am not, in a classic sense, a change management consultant. But on a number of projects, I have had to take on the assignment as the change management lead.

And, of course, I have worked with and been exposed to many organizational change management professionals working along side them on complex optimization and transformation projects.

I have learned a lot over the years and continue to be educated on the science of change on all my projects.

It's interesting that, while regularly misunderstood and often maligned, organizational change management is critical to the success of any optimization or transformation project.

When you are undertaking a business process optimization/transformation project, the organizational change management workstream provides the "glue" to bring the various parts of the organization together with a common understanding of the goals and objectives of the project.

Change only happens when led by the top executives of the organization who must not only lead and support the change program but who also must walk the walk and talk the talk and be an integral part of the change journey.

We all are resistant to change. Even professionals who are change agents, like me, are resistant to change in certain parts of our lives. My job has been and continues to be "make change happen," yet I am rooted in my own personal behaviors where I am totally resistant to change.

My behavioral norms have been developed over decades of living. I like to do certain things the way I like to do them. And don't ask me to change just for the sake of changing.

It always gets down to "What's in it for Me?" where "ME" is the key.

In this book, I have talked about the various roles that I play in a project and have maintained that half of the work I do is as a Psychologist. This is all orchestrated by my role as the Conductor.

A Culture of Change

Before we get into a discussion on what I have done on current and past projects, let's ask the question: Is there a better way to handle Organizational Change Management?

I will defer to the experts in this field, but it seems to me that we need to be working on developing an organizational culture that is adaptable to change, not resistant to change — an organization that is resilient in the face of change.

And to do so, should we be looking to getting away from organizational change management as some discrete event related to a project and build change into the fabric or the DNA of the organization to create a culture of change.

In my opinion, organizations are going to have to learn to adapt to change as part of their DNA and build the agility and flexibility to handle change in all levels of the organization, from the C-suite to the shop floor.

The old adage is the change starts from The Top. I believe this will continue to be true.

But C-suite executives will have to show more resiliency to the organization in the way they communicate and adapt to change themselves. "Do As I Say, Not As I Do" doesn't work.

The mindset for change must evolve in the organization from a mentality to fight change to a mentality to embrace and adopt change. This is a fundamental reorientation of the cultures of most companies.

The mindset for change must evolve in the organization from a mentality to fight change to a mentality to embrace and adopt change. This is a fundamental reorientation of the cultures of most companies.

Change cannot be left up to Human Resources to lead alone. The entire organization must be educated and trained on how to embrace change vs. fight change as it adapts and transforms to a culture of change.

Getting On and Off the Highway

When discussing the adoption of change, I use the analogy of getting on and off the highway to showcase the concept of speed.

When getting on a highway, there is an entrance ramp.

The goal is to come up to highway speed so that you can merge into traffic smoothly.

Some people timidly step on the accelerator. They never come up to highway speed, and the merge is cumbersome.

Some people "press the pedal to the metal" and rapidly accelerate, even at speeds that exceed the traffic flow. These people zip onto the highway, and off they go.

But on average, most people gradually increase their acceleration to meet the posted highway speed and seamlessly merge into traffic.

Worst-case scenarios include the drivers who STOP at the end of the ramp and wait for an opening to merge onto the highway. (Just saying, but I usually drive around them as I am going FAST.)

On the exit ramp, the objective is to decelerate.

Some people start gently braking at the beginning of the exit ramp and crawl to a stop at the end of the ramp.

Others fly down the exit ramp and slam on the brakes near the very end. You see them coming in the rear-view mirror and wonder if they are going to rear-end you.

But on average, people take their foot off the accelerator to gradually decelerate, brake about halfway down the ramp and keep riding their brakes to the end of the ramp.

Worst-case scenario are the ones who SLAM on the brakes at the beginning of the ramp and you almost rear-end them.

What is your acceleration and deceleration profile? I am fast getting on and gradual getting off.

This is how people change: fast, gradual, crawl and slam.

I was once given the following distribution that describes how people change.

No matter what you say or do:

- 20 % is for you (fast)
- 20% are against you (slam)
- The middle 60% are undecided (gradual and crawl)

The battleground for change management is the 60% in the middle, aka the undecided.

How many of them can you get on board to support the project?

The elements of the five stages of grief will also take hold here.

If you are in the top 20% and gung-ho (fast) on the project, your denial and anger will show up in the form of frustration with the bottom 20% over their lack of support. You are already at acceptance for the project, but you can't believe the bottom 20 %, the strong resisters, don't share your same excitement.

If you are in the bottom 20% (slam) and totally resistant to the project, your denial and anger is real and can be extreme. I don't care what you say or do, I will not be convinced the project is a good idea. Unfortunately, these people are very dangerous to the success of the project.

They may not be providing a frontal assault, but they might be actually working behind the scenes to be very subversive, and influence others with their negative mindset to derail the project.

The 60% battleground people are the ones who change gradually or at a crawl. They are in the negotiating stage of the five stages of grief. They have gotten through denial and anger and are now looking to find out "What's in it for me?" These employees are the ones you have to win over! They are the employees the bottom 20% is trying to influence with their negative mindset.

When you ask a client if they have a track record of being good at change management, they'll say, "Oh yeah, sure." Then when you ask them about how the implementations of major projects have gone relative to organizational acceptance, they will be hard-pressed to find one project that went well.

"How did that last acquisition integration go?"

"It was and is a disaster. We have yet to get over the cultural conflicts."

Be prepared for this client to fight you tooth and nail that a change management workstream is required.

Change Management Workstream Resistance

Whether a project is with a client or an internal project, many organizations are resistant to the change management workstream.

And rightfully so as some of the leaders may have had a bad experience with change management. Trust me; there are many of those.

What I will discuss in this chapter is how I handle organizational change management. I will show you how I use some of the tools that are found in change management. It's not so much the tools, but how they are used and applied, that makes the difference between success and failure.

When does change management start on a project? Well, it depends.

Many times, I am brought into a project after the organization has decided that it needs to make some changes. In some cases, when I show up, the project has a name, the steering committee has been selected, and the project manager has been assigned.

If a company is this far along, there usually have been rumblings through the grapevine that something is up. Some negative effects of change management through "indirect communication" are starting to filter through the organization through unfounded rumors. "Water cooler discussions" are taking place.

Many in the organization know something is up. Stories about the project have been created, which in many cases are false. Unfounded theories are being presented as to what the project means and who will be impacted.

So now the steering committee, project manager and project team have to deal with "fake news."

Fake news has such a negative effect on the project, organization and project teams. But this is the reality I have to live with on most projects: digging out of a change management hole.

I much prefer being brought into a project during the ideation stage. It is much better to work with the client or internal sponsor to define the project upfront and have a communication plan in place to start the execution early on/before the rumors start!

As you can see, negative change management can start very fast with fake news filtering and percolating through the organization.

If fake news is already out there, then there is an urgency to get the communication plan established and a conversation started with the organization. Pronto! We'll discuss communication later in the chapter.

Now that we have set the stage around some of the more interesting aspects of organizational change management let's get into the process that I use.

Strategic Initiatives

Whether I am coming in during the ideation stage or an already defined project, one of the most important first steps for me is to understand what strategic initiatives the organization is working on and where the project falls within the initiatives.

If you remember the balanced scorecard discussion, the strategic initiatives related to the high-level corporate objectives the organization would focus on for a year or two.

These focuses fall into four categories:

- Customer
- Learning and innovation
- Internal process
- Financial

I want to know the distribution of the strategic initiatives into the four categories.

And I want to know what category this project falls into and whether there are any cause and effect relationships stemming from the other corporate objectives, and initiatives.

It won't surprise you to read that not everyone will be on the same page relative to which balanced scorecard category the project will fall into. Let alone where all the initiatives fall.

This step is critical to achieving executive alignment. If the executive team and/or the steering committee are not on the same page, then this is where the change management troubles can begin.

Another issue you will run across during this analysis is that sometimes, companies or your organization will bite off more than they can chew.

The organization can only handle so much change. This is another classic failure mode for projects.

People get fatigued by high-intensity projects. Even two high-intensity projects can be draining on organization resilience.

This fatigue can be compounded when certain people are asked to be part of two projects.

And they also are being asked to keep doing their normal day job!

This is where you really need to understand the big picture of what's going on in the organization around the strategic initiatives and how the project intersects with other strategic initiatives.

Sales & Operations Planning (S&OP) / Integrated Business Planning (IBP) Example

I've assisted multiple clients, large and small, on S&OP transformation programs.

Let's look at what I have learned from these S&OP projects, which are very significant transformation programs.

S&OP and IBP are an end-to-end business management methodology that transforms how a company operates.

Strategic Initiative

Typically, if a company is planning to implement S&OP or IBP, it is their #1 or #2 strategic initiative.

Steering committees for S&OP/IBP projects are made up of the president/CEO (executive sponsor) and C-suite/executive senior vice presidents from R&D, sales, marketing, supply chain, manufacturing operations, finance, information technology and HR.

S&OP/IBP is truly a cross-functional business management methodology.

I enjoy working with early – to mid-career, up-and-coming leaders who have been nominated by a number of members of the steering committee to lead these important initiatives. And in many cases, I have been fortunate to collaborate with a number of these professionals.

The client project manager and I jointly develop a set of questions we were going to ask the steering committee relative to the project, to gain their understanding of S&OP/IBP and how they would define success.

Balanced Scorecard Category

One of the questions I always ask is which balanced scorecard category best represented why the project is so important to the organization.

- Is the project focused on improving the customer experience?
- Is the project focused on improving learning and innovation?
- Is the project focused on improving internal processes?
- Is the project focused on improving financial performance?

As you can imagine, in round one, you will receive responses for all four questions: customer, learning and innovation, internal process and financial.

And to be fair, S&OP/IBP projects are going to impact all these categories. But which one is the true driving force for this particular S&O/IBPP project?

Round two is a joint meeting with the steering committee where we play back the steering committee's responses in an open discussion. There are no right or wrong answers. We are being the detectives, looking for clues to the mystery of why the organization wants to implement S&OP/IBP.

Note: I have mentioned this before, but when you are starting a big optimization or transformation project, it is important to see how the steering committee members interact with each other and how they come to a consensus on decisions.

These are usually excellent collaborative discussions led by the project manager and me as the conductor.

Having a Human Resources executive as a member of the steering committee is very important because S&OP/IBP has a huge impact on the organization. New positions are created, old positions are retired, significant changes in job responsibilities occur.

During the discussion with the executive sponsor and steering committee, the consensus of the executives is that the S&OP/IBP project is aligned with the Balanced Scorecard category of Learning and Innovation.

The S&OP/IBP project is the #2 strategic initiative the company is focused on after their #1 strategic initiative, Integrated Globalization.

The steering committee has now approved that the S&OP/IBP project a learning and innovation initiative that is required to support the strategy for Integrated Globalization.

We now understand how our S&OP/IBP project fits into in the big picture of what the organization is focused on for the next few years,

Themes for Success

Themes for Success is one of my major go-to artifacts for organizational change management.

When developing the themes for success, I am working toward executive/leadership/steering committee alignment.

To get to this point early on in the projects helps in so many elements of organizational change management.

It means I now have the executive/leadership/steering committee aligned on the objectives of the project.

And that means we now have the basis for how we will define success.

This is a great communication tool to get the entire organization aligned with the objectives of the project.

No more ambiguity is allowed as we have created clearly defined objectives.

When we send out communication to the organization around project status, I prefer to have the Themes for Success as the first thing everyone sees in the communication. I like to keep reinforcing the message.

Under strategic initiatives, we now know that the S&OP/IBP project is the #2 strategic initiative for the organization. It is totally aligned with the #1 strategic initiative, Integrated Globalization.

We have worked with the executive/leadership/steering committee to determine that the S&OP/IBP project is focused on learning and innovation to be able to deliver Integrated Globalization.

We have worked with the executive/leadership/steering committee to define the Themes for Success for the S&OP Project. We can share the Themes for Success with the project team to educate and align on the project goals. We can share the Themes for Success with the broader organization to educate and align on project goals and the expectations for the organization.

Example: Project Themes for Success

- A new sustainable XXXXXX process is an absolute requirement for us to achieve our strategic growth vision.

- We must educate and train our teams to support a new world class XXXXXX process. Roles & Responsibilities will be clearly defined so that we as an organization are all on the same page.
- The new XXXXXX process must be designed to allow us to execute with the flexibility needed to support our various global businesses. This flexibility will enable our team to effectively manage YYYYYY.
- The decisions resulting from the new XXXXXX process must be quantifiable and fact based. The organization must work from "One Version of the Truth".
- The new XXXXXX process is a Bold change management initiative as we transform our organization into a global leader.
- The Leadership Team will lead by example as we all must embrace the change for the collective good of our individual stakeholders and the organization.
- The new XXXXXX process must be viewed as a competitive advantage for our strategic growth, not as a barrier or hindrance to our success.

Change Champions

In review, Change Champions are highly regarded employees of the organization included as extended members of the project team that work to facilitate the changes required to make the project successful.

They are influential leaders of the organization that are well respected.

The Change Champion is a formal member of the Organization Change Management Workstream.

They are educated on the project vision, trained to become proactive advocates and mobilized within the organization to lead change.

There can be multiple levels of Change Champions on an Optimization or Transformation project, from Executives to the Shop Floor.

You need to select your Change Champions carefully as they are the eyes and ears of the Project Team inside of the organization.

Change Champions are asked to sense the pulse of the impacts of change on the organization as they are well respected and trusted by their peers.

They share their finds with the Project Team to make sure there are clear channels of communications with the organization.

I like to identify the Executive/Leadership/Steering Committee as Executive Change Champions.

Executives are the primary conduit for communications to the organization. They set the vision and direction for the project.

Changes comes from the top; consequentially these leaders are your most strategic and influential Change Champions.

Stating the obvious, Executive Change Champions play a critical role on the project.

I like to make sure I reinforce the roles that executive play as Executive Change Champions on the project.

Ownership, Communication and Discipline

Do you also remember the group development model: Forming, Storming, Norming, Performing?

The executive/leadership/steering committee will be going through these phases of group development for the project.

Has this executive/leadership/steering committee been together before on other optimization or transformation projects?

Good, they may already be in the Performing stage.

If not, they will have to progress through Forming, Storming, Norming and Performing.

Progression through the group development models is required for executives to be successful in the next concept we will discuss.

What I have found is that executives must embrace the following three principles for the project to be successful.

- Ownership
- Communication
- Discipline

Executives need to own the project, meaning they have a responsibility to the organization to be an active participant.

If they only give the project lip service, that attitude will filter down through their organization.

Unfortunately, their directors and managers will start giving lip service to the project, too.

When executives show a lack of ownership and active participation in the project, the message is clearly sent to the rest of the organization and the project can hit some major hurdles, even collapse.

The subsequent collateral damage that is inflicted on the organization is very damaging.

Lack of executive engagement and ownership is one of the classic examples of why S&OP/IBP and other transformation programs fail.

Shifting to communication, it is incredibly important that executives are all on the same page with consistent communication.

Conflicting messaging and communication to the organization lead to high levels of confusion.

You will see that this is a top priority for me with executives: getting them on the same page.

The project requires clear, concise and consistent communication.

And finally discipline, because optimization and transformation projects are not for the faint of heart.

They take a lot of work and discipline.

As an example, If the organization had not implemented updated information technology in 10 years, well, it's going to take discipline to implement the new systems.

If an organization has left processes unattended for 10 years and they have morphed into a big mess, it's going to take discipline to right the ship.

Optimization and transformation projects take discipline. Lots of discipline.

In our S&OP/IBP example, lack of discipline is a contributing factor to many failed S&OP/IBP projects. The executives and organization lack the discipline to implement and maintain S&OP/IBP.

Lack of executive ownership, poor or inconsistent communication, and lack of discipline bring optimization and transformation programs to failure mode very rapidly.

> **Lack of executive ownership, poor or inconsistent communication, and lack of discipline bring optimization and transformation programs to failure mode very rapidly.**

Own it. Communicate effectively. Maintain discipline.

60-Second Elevator Pitch

I have found it very helpful to develop a 60-second elevator pitch for change champions to use for less formal, more intimate conversations with people.

Developed by the project team and approved by the steering committee, we'll use the following example of a 60-second elevator pitch the change champions will use when discussing the project: "The S&OP/IBP project is a significant investment in learning and innovation as we grow toward integrated globalization. The S&OP/IBP project will educate and train the entire organization on new, innovative principles to manage our complicated business processes. The benefits of a robust S&OP/IBP process will be felt from the board room to the shop floor."

If the water cooler conversations have already started, we have to "nip them in the bud" right away. We cannot afford fake news to continue to percolate through the organization.

The 60-second elevator pitch is an excellent tool for the change champions network to use for communication to the employees they interact with on a daily basis.

The Bottom 20%

So far it has all been "kumbaya" with the executive/leadership/ steering committee.

Do you remember the: 20 % is for you, 20% is against you and the middle 60% is undecided?

I'm sorry to say; you will find this distribution in the executive/leadership/steering committee as well.

If executive/leadership/steering committee has eight members, there may be one or two on the committee who are against the project. It's nothing personal, but sometimes it is.

You may have an executive who you view as an executive change champion, and the situation is just the opposite! They are anything but a change champion!

If you have a few committee members against the project, hopefully going through the strategic initiative discussion and Themes for Success development will clean up the bottom 20%.

But unfortunately, hope is not a strategy!

To get to their levels of responsibility and authority within the organization, they have to be very good at what they do or wear Teflon suits.

Teflon suits mean nothing sticks to them. The people who wear these suits often have others looking on wondering how they have gotten into that position in the organization.

The Teflon suits can be very dangerous on a project if they are in the bottom 20%.

The executive sponsor and other executive/leadership/steering committee members really need to work to get any subversive players into line.

We need executive change champions that are all working for the good of the project.

Educating the Core and Extended Teams

The project can have core and extended project teams.

The core project team is led by the project manager and a group of say, six individuals. In our S&OP/IBP example, the team would be made up of one person from marketing, sales, supply chain, manufacturing operations, and finance and information technology.

The extended team is an expanded cross-section of additional representatives from R&D, marketing, sales, supply chain, manufacturing operations, finance and IT, who would be responsible for various parts of the S&OP/IBP process.

After the ballyhoo of the kickoff meeting, we need to get down to the business of educating the core and extended teams on leading practices of S&OP/IBP and Themes for Success.

The importance of educating the teams on leading practices and Themes for Success is a critical first step in the next level down of change champions.

Not everyone on either the core or extended teams may be knowledgeable about the transformation area. You need to educate them, and it may take multiple education sessions to get the teams to where they feel confident.

If you can arrange to have a few members of the steering committee (Executive Change Champions) attend these education sessions, it greatly reinforces their ownership and discipline to the project. They are communicating their support.

You may have a false sense of security stemming from the education sessions going well complete with a lot of good questions and good audience participation.

When you start up the following week, the project manager will pull you aside and ask that you go through the educational materials again with the core team. No problem, that's what we are here for, getting everyone educated.

Then, you'll go through the education session again. When you do, you will likely be surprised by some of the questions that come from the core team and the project manager.

They did struggle with some of the concepts of leading practices and Themes for Success.

You will come to learn over time that this is not unusual with large optimization and transformation projects.

Note: Large optimization and transformation projects are complicated. It is not unusual that you have to continually educate on the concepts. Think of the on-ramp and off-ramp example; people learn at different speeds/paces. When you get to the training stage, plan on multiple training sessions.

In one of my S&OP projects, we held multiple education sessions with the core team on the leading practices of S&OP.

The company had implemented S&OP on their own and knew they were floundering.

The core team and I sat in on an S&OP meeting.

The core team was not part of the existing S&OP process. They were a new team assembled to re-implement S&OP the correct way.

During the meeting, I was observing the core team.

They all had the proverbial "deer in the headlights" look.

After the meeting I asked a question to break the ice: "Well, that was very informative. What do you think?"

One of the core team members responded, "We've got a lot of work to do. Whatever they want to call that, the current process is not S&OP. Not in the way you would traditionally define S&OP. It does not even vaguely represent how an S&OP meeting should function. This just seems like just a big bitching session with finger-pointing and nothing getting resolved."

Our education sessions worked! The core team grasped the leading practices and could clearly differentiate between the leading practices and how the current S&OP process was functioning.

Unlearning

One of the biggest challenges you have with an optimization or transformation project is not learning new ways to do things; it's unlearning how things have been done for years

Unlearning the old ways can, for some, be harder than learning the new ways.

Like muscle memory, people have mind memory.

You'll educate and train these team members on the new ways to do things, but when push comes to shove, they'll revert back to their old practices and behaviors because this is the way they have done it in the past. They rely on the old practices in many cases because they are still not confident with the new practices.

In the example I referenced above, one of the biggest challenges we faced was for the organization to unlearn what they considered to be S&OP.

Performance Management

I like to work with the project teams to develop the KPIs and metrics for S&OP/IBP.

S&OP/IBP pretty well follows the Extended SCOR model.

I am using it to show the distribution of 16 of the KPIs in the KPI matrix on page 270.

Note: I have on occasion, broken out the "Sell" KPI into "Sales" and "Marketing" as two separate areas of performance indication. Whichever works best should be the path taken.

Don't be surprised that when you start to work with the project teams, you'll hear about problems with their reporting system.

The reporting system does not support the accurate development of the KPIs and metrics

KPI Distribution

	Financial	Customer	Internal Process	Learning & Innovation
Innovate			New Product Time to Market	
Sell		Global Market Penetration		
Plan	Working Capital			Forecast & BIAS Accuracy
Source	Raw Material Costs		Supplier Scorecards	
Make	Manufacturing Costs		Manufacturing Efficiencies	Manufacturing Efficiencies
Deliver	Logistic Costs	On Time in Full (OTIF)		
Service		Customer Scorecards		
Return	Logistic Costs		RMA Process	

Surprise, it often is the result of poor data quality and governance.

The project teams may agree that these are the correct KPIs to govern S&OP, but they have little to no faith that their reporting system will support their needs.

This can be very frustrating as we've discussed.

Project teams will feel they can't truly progress in putting forth their best transformation program when the reporting systems do not meet their needs.

This has to be brought up to the steering committee.

Hopefully, a transformation program will get the organization off the dime and address their data quality and governance reporting issues.

Communication Plan

Having a solid approach to organizational communication is very important in creating a successful optimization or transformation project.

If the water cooler conversations have already started, we have to "nip them in the bud" right away. We cannot afford fake news to percolate through the organization. Leaders are the ones to get that message across.

During the monthly steering committee meeting, you will present your plans for the monthly S&OP project newsletter.

The repetitive monthly cycle with a newsletter always begins with a message from the president and/or the steering committee. It reinforces to everyone in the organization that the project status is coming from the very top of the organization.

As mentioned, I always start with the Themes for Success, followed by the president's message and then an update on the project timeline identifying progress to date and highlighting activities for the next month.

This can be a different approach for your company or a client.

Many do not have a monthly communication going out to the organization in general, never mind a communication dedicated to optimization or transformation projects.

They are constantly dealing with water cooler conversations and fake news.

The monthly newsletter can be a refreshing approach to the organization.

Another approach that I have found very effective is conducting periodic checkpoint meetings with employees called among other things, a town hall meeting.

The executives become storytellers by sharing how they struggled with change on large projects, made the investment in themselves (i.e., got uncomfortable), and ultimately came out successful and on top.

Building belief in your organization that the way we must accept change is through personal stories will reinforce the message that we are all working toward a path to a better working environment.

I remember years ago at an annual meeting; our president said that communication to the organization was going to be one of his highest priorities for the coming year.

A few weeks later, we heard from outside sources that the company had made a significant acquisition.

Low and behold, it was true.

The president sent out a company-wide email with his tail between his legs. (This is what made him an endearing leader). "How could I have screwed up so quickly with my communication goal?" His blurb in the newsletter read. "I failed to let our organization know about the acquisition before the news got out. My apologies. This will never happen again as long as I am your president".

Organization Impact

As you can well imagine and have probably felt, optimization and transformation projects have a significant impact on the organization.

As the change management SME on a project, I use some of the tools for impact assessment and organization design.

S&OP/IBP is a transformation project which is an end-to-end business management system.

As you dive deeper into the guts of S&OP/IBP, the impact on the organization and the realization of the project teams become much more visible.

In change management, there is a concept called "the valley of despair."

I would describe "the valley of despair" as the low point on the change management emotional journey where the task at hand may feel insurmountable.

The change management emotional journey starts with optimism, progresses to pessimism, hits rock bottom with despair/skepticism, struggles to acceptance, and then returns to optimism.

Like the five stages of grief, the valley of despair happens periodically during our everyday lives as we live through a variety of life experiences.

Getting your bachelor's degree or MBA, the realities of a new job, hiking up a steep trail, lowering your golf handicap, the first years of marriage, all of these experiences, although seemingly good on the outside, can still elicit feelings of despair.

The depression stage of the five stages of grief and the valley of despair are very similar in context.

The challenge is helping the client through the valley of despair so that they do not linger in despair too long.

Because in a project transformation project, despair will happen repeatedly.

First, the project team hits despair as they understand the daunting tasks at hand.

Then, the steering committee can hit a level of despair if they believe they have bitten off more than they can chew.

Further, as you roll out the project to the organization, the organization hits despair, too. *Wow, this is a lot of work*! They might be thinking.

This is why we need discipline!

Transformation projects are not a walk in the park.

I will not profess that I am an expert in this area, but I have worked on enough projects to know that I can never let optimism leave the client.

Even when I can feel some sense of despair myself.

I have to be honest with the client, but I also have to maintain a strong sense of optimism.

Have I ever experienced the valley of despair when the realization hit that the organization will never succeed in the project?

Yes, I have been there.

When I feel this way, my job then is to be very detailed and honest as to why I think the project will fail.

I have to have concrete examples to first share with the project teams and then the steering committee about exactly why I see the project failing.

This means there are very difficult discussions to be had with the project manager, project teams and steering committee.

But sometimes they have to be had, and the circumstances may be totally out of your control.

A good example is what I mentioned before. When the company has multiple high-intensity projects going on at the same time. This is a classic failure mode for projects.

This is where you really need to understand the big picture of what's going on in the organization around strategic initiatives and how the project intersects with other strategic initiatives.

I have had to explain to a steering committee that two projects are draining resources on our project and then ask if they could provide some prioritization.

If no changes to priorities are made, then don't be surprised that both projects will get a grade of C.

For example, I was brought into a transformation project in the ideation stage, where we spent two months building a very detailed project plan.

During this time, as we were interacting with the various teams, we came to the realization that this company did not have enough organizational depth and A-Team players to make the project a success.

They just did not have enough people to run their business and staff with a transformation project of this magnitude.

This was going to be a multi-year project, worth a lot of money, but we had to be honest with ourselves and the steering committee that the project was a disaster in the making.

The impact on the organization would have been catastrophic.

We presented our findings to the steering committee.

You know the drill; the five stages of grief took hold pretty fast with denial and anger setting in during the briefing.

They had sold the project to the board of directors, and now we were telling them that our opinion was that their organization, in its current state, was not ready for the project.

Over the next few weeks as the steering committee worked its way through negotiating and depression, we built an organization plan for the path forward with very specific recommendations.

After we presented the plan for the path to the steering committee; it took them some time to get to acceptance.

The steering committee was then prepared to go to the board with a revised plan.

The board reluctantly agreed to delay the project and did provide funding for the new organization.

It may take the company a year or more to restart the project.

But at the end of the day, they have now structured the organization with the right staffing for the project to be a success.

This leads us to a more detailed discussion on organization design.

Organization Design

Organization design is an area of importance on optimization and transformation projects.

Our work in the current state to the future state will highlight the critical nature of organization design.

We will need to assess the current organization to determine if they have the skills required to be successful in future state roles and responsibilities.

We will be identifying gaps in the current skill sets of the organization.

There will be new skills required for future state roles and responsibilities.

Let me discuss a few examples from S&OP/IBP.

The S&OP/IBP Process Owner owns, manages and coordinates the end-to-end S&OP/IBP process.

It is a position of significant responsibility, and important to the success of S&OP/IBP.

When you evaluate the existing organization, is there a person or two who stands out as a possible S&OP/IBP Process Owner?

The person must be well-versed in the entire business, and very well respected up and down the organization.

They must be mature, trustworthy and viewed as a leader with a good head on their shoulders.

They must be very organized.

They cannot be a pushover by any means and must have the ability to listen, collaborate and bring about meaningful decisions and change.

If you are fortunate, the organization will select a candidate or two to fill this very important role.

Once the candidates have been identified, it can be hard work to get the person to accept the position of responsibility as S&OP/IBP Process Owner.

This is a very demanding and politically sensitive role.

As part of any large transformation project, the organization assessment and design are critical to the long-term success and viability of the project.

Process Simulation

As part of education and training, I like to hold process simulation workshops.

In our S&OP/IBP example, I like to bring all the participants in the S&OP/IBP process to a workshop where we simulate the end-to-end S&OP/IBP meetings.

This is where the S&OP/IBP Process Owner gets their feet wet with the new teams and processes.

I think sometimes they feel like they have been thrown into the deep end!

During the simulations, we'll focus on highlighting the hand-offs between the different process steps and teams.

We'll work to determine if there are any gaps in the information handed off to the next process step.

This has worked very effectively as all of the teams can see how the different meetings flowed together into a well-orchestrated S&OP/IBP process.

We will end the workshop where the teams are tasked to resolve and develop corrective actions to reconcile the issues/problems that were identified in the simulation.

The S&OP/IBP Process Owner lead the reconciliation process.

The next day, we will have a follow-up workshop where we will review the corrective actions the teams have developed.

During the second half of the next steering committee meeting, the S&OP Process Owner will lead the simulation of the executive S&OP/IBP meeting.

This simulation educates the steering committee on the dynamics of the executive S&OP/IBP meeting as many, if not, all will be part of the meeting going forward.

During the preparing for implementation stage of the project, we'll go through a few simulations, as mastering any new process like S&OP/IBP is positively an iterative learning process.

The Rank and File

We've talked about how projects impact skilled positions, but what about the rank and file?

These are the foot soldiers of the organization: R&D, marketing, sales, supply chain, manufacturing operations, finance and HR.

In many ways, these people are the most affected by the project because when they ask the question, "What is in it for me?" the answer can be "Not much" or "Nothing."

Their jobs are going to be impacted by a new system, new processes and new reporting lines, and they are asked to or instructed just to go along.

We can explain to them that this is good for the company, and the right thing to do, as well as the fact that they might pick up some new skills and technologies.

For them, it means having to learn a new process or system and unlearn what they have been doing for years.

I'm just being honest here. I've seen huge levels of indifference on multiple projects.

All the institutional and tribal knowledge is being thrown out the door with a big thud!

All the work centers around tricks, the secret Excel spreadsheets, and the notes in a book that is 10 years old — the hidden factories.

You are familiarized with the acronym ERP and that, for our purposes, it has meant Enterprise Resource Planning.

Well, there is another translation: Early Retirement Program.

Meaning some people will never be able to step up to the new system or new processes.

They are so rooted in the ways they have been doing their job; they have no interest or ability to change.

Some will say that these are the "old farts" in the organization and in many cases this is true.

But trust me when I tell you I have seen younger employees with no interest or ability to change. This is not a generational issue.

Many in that bottom 20% representing those who are against anything and everything about the new system or process know they are exposed and afraid.

In my experience, the key to working with the rank and file is to educate, reinforce the message and provide a lot of training, early and often.

Repetitive education and training have worked well for me.

Some will say the organization doesn't have time for all the education and training.

Only time will tell.

Change champions are in place to be the eyes and ears of the project team. It is their responsibility to make sure they understand the pulse of the organization.

During the education and training, the change champions and trainers must pay close attention to the feedback they are receiving.

Who is getting the new process or system right away? Who is struggling? Who is totally lost?

If you remember the end-to-end process flow from the information technology chapter, it is a tool we used to educate and train the rank and file.

As you can see again on page 283, the process flows from customer service to demand planning to production planning to procurement to production to quality to shipping.

This is an integrated process flow to educate the departments that they are dependent on the department before them to transact properly. The department after them is dependent on *them* to transact properly.

The entire process is sequenced to flow in an integrated set of transactions.

We use this flow as part of our education to reinforce with the teams that everyone is in this together and that any "weak link" will throw off the entire process.

We want to make sure that users understand their responsibilities to their teams and other team members from different departments.

You cannot reinforce this message enough. This flow has helped get this message across very clearly.

Any ERP system is a series of transactions. As an example, SAP does a very good job documenting the transaction with specific transaction codes such as MD63, MD04 and ZFORMULA.

This is where the trainers modify the generic flow to SAP or Oracle-specific for a particular job function.

The transactions show the users what they need to perform to complete their daily jobs.

Discrete Manufacturing Process Flow

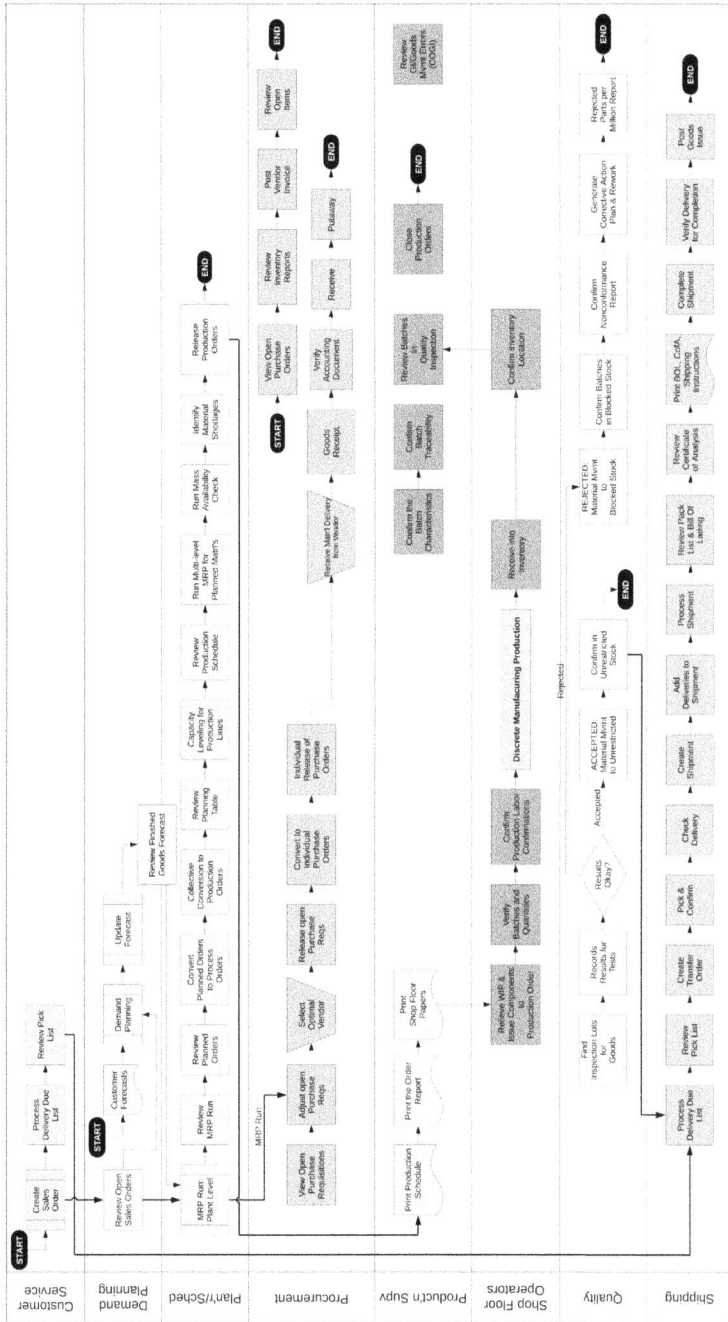

Demand & Production Planning Discrete

In this example on page 284, we would put in the SAP transactions' codes for the demand planners and production planners.

We worked to make this as clear as possible for the users. And this worked out very effectively during training.

Readiness Assessment

I've seen a number of implementations Go Live, even with what was considered "adequate training," and the rank and file are just not prepared to handle the new world.

There needs to be a readiness assessment after training and before Go Live to make sure all levels of the organization are ready to take on the new process or system.

I like to see integration testing done simultaneously with some end-user testing on a number of test cases.

Test cases are a real-world, end-to-end set of transactions used to determine whether the technology and organization are working properly.

The successful passing of integration and end-user testing is a critical, true self-assessment led by the project team and change champions to provide a final validation that all systems are go!

Organization readiness is as important as system readiness!

The Bottom 20%

In my experience, this population needs direct communication about where they stand.

Either these employees are "with the program or against the program." We can't afford any "shades of gray" here.

Unfortunately, these employees can be very divisive and destructive and drag a project down.

We can be sensitive and empathetic to their feelings as some of my Change Management colleagues have expressed, but the reality is that everyone needs to get on the same page.

As I have mentioned before, and fair warning, some of the 20% can be on the steering committee. This can and will cause a lot of problems.

If this is true and they share their negativity with their organization/department, this can poison an entire business function.

This behavior really needs to be addressed directly with the specific employee, maybe through some one-on-one counseling.

Summary

In the organizational change management chapter, we have discussed:

- A culture of change
- Getting on and off the highway
- Change management workstream resistance
- Strategic initiatives
- Themes for success
- Change champions
- Ownership, communication and discipline
- 60-second elevator pitch
- The bottom 20%

- Educating the core and extended teams
- Unlearning
- Performance management
- Communication
- Organization impact and design
- Process simulation
- Rank and file
- Readiness assessment
- The bottom 20%

Of course, I have only touched on some of the key elements in each one of these focus areas of organizational change management.

And hopefully, you have read about enough useful examples and anecdotal stories to emphasize some of the critical issues that can be experienced on your projects.

Organization change management is a complex area of any project.

Change as a preference in a person's life is not in most people's DNA.

But the fact of the matter is change happens all the time.

It is how you approach and manage change, whether in a project or your personal life that matters.

The five stages of grief and the change journey can coexist in the world of change.

People can experience the five stages of grief and the change journey at the same time.

I won't profess myself to be the expert of organizational change management.

Many professionals make this their business. So there are many experts.

I'll be interested to see how the experts develop their approaches to develop a culture of change.

But I have witnessed good, and bad organizational change management approaches in my projects.

If I don't have a change management workstream and a professional on the project, then I have to look at what I have learned over the years and apply those lessons as best I can to the situation at hand.

Of course, I've made my mistakes. Everyone does.

But I do try my best to make the organizational change management experience the very best that it can be for all involved.

CHAPTER 9

ARTIFICIAL INTELLIGENCE, MACHINE LEARNING, ROBOTIC PROCESS OPTIMIZATION, PREDICTIVE AND PRESCRIPTIVE ANALYTICS

I would like to thank Gregory North, President of Global North, for his valuable insights included in this chapter. Greg is a recognized thought leader in artificial intelligence (AI) and digital transformation.

I would like to thank Robert (Rob) Sadar, Co-Founder of Anno.AI for his valuable insights included in the chapter. Rob is a recognized thought leader in AI.

Now, let's talk about the crux of this chapter.

I am not sure what I have heard of most these days, the cloud or AI.

Either way, both cloud-computing and AI are getting a lot of air time as companies work to position themselves as leaders and early adopters of these advanced technologies.

Every 5-10 years, there is a quantum leap in technology when the hardware, software, data and knowledge catch up with the vision.

That is where we are today with artificial intelligence, machine learning (ML), robotic process automation (RPA) and prescriptive analytics (PA).

If you have been in technology long enough, you know that Artificial Intelligence, Machine Learning, Robotic Process Automation and Prescriptive Analytics is evolutionary not revolutionary.

Many of the same challenges we have faced in the past will need to be addressed today and in the near future as AI, ML, RPA and PA becomes more main stream and adoption begins to accelerate.

And in many cases the challenges will be magnified.

Definitions

A few definitions to start around AI, ML RPA and predictive and prescriptive analytics.

AI is intelligence demonstrated by machines. An AI machine has the ability to interpret data, learn from the data, and use the learnings to achieve specific goals and tasks.

ML is the use of algorithms and statistical models that allow computers to perform a task without instructions. ML is considered a subset of AI. ML algorithms build mathematical models to make predictions or decisions without being programmed.

Robotic process automation (RPA) is the technology with a "robot," which will capture and interpret applications to execute a business process or processes with one or more digital technology systems. RPA robots utilize the user interface to capture data and manipulate the data and applications. RPA can handle simple processes or integrate multiple processes across multiple department.

Predictive analytics is a form of advanced analytics used to make predictions about unknown future events. Predictive analytics uses a variety of statistical techniques such as data mining, predictive modeling and ML. Predictive analytics analyzes current and historical data to make predictions.

Prescriptive analytics is the third and final phase of business analytics, which also includes descriptive and predictive analytics. Referred to as the "final frontier of analytic capabilities," prescriptive analytics entails the application of mathematical and computational sciences and suggests decision options to take advantage of the results of descriptive and predictive analytics.

My Personal History

Let me provide a brief history of my experiences with AI, ML and PA.

I led a team that created a propriety software system to help manage our rapidly growing outsourcing business.

The outsourcing model was focused operational excellence in large industrial manufacturing plants.

The outsourcing model included services in the acquisition and management of MRO materials, laboratory, engineering and environmental services.

Our software consisted of multiple modules such as procurement, inventory control, quality, engineering and financial.

The system was built on a common data model, meaning all the modules fed the same database, which was partitioned for the different modules.

One of the modules was for quality control (QC).

Multiple samples were tested during the day across a variety of machines in the plant with the results (data) for each test entered into the QC module.

Another module, for engineering, was a mapping of the manufacturing plant that captured various attributes for all of the pieces of equipment in the plant.

Over time, as we collected more and more data, we were able to build analytic models to predict future failure modes for the parts and machines.

In the advanced analytic model, if we had two different plants with the same type of equipment, from the same manufacturer, producing the same parts, we had the ability to predict the future performance of each machine in the different plants.

The advanced analytics is one of the areas that separated us from our competition.

The advanced analytics were developed by our engineers.

When I joined Oracle, I was introduced to the new demand planning, advanced supply chain planning and business intelligence solutions.

I really enjoyed playing around with the demand planner.

I was not responsible for the demand planning solution.

But I had a real interest in being educated and trained on the demand planner for my own personal growth.

I can't remember exactly, but the demand planner at the time came with maybe nine algorithmic models to calculate future demand.

These included average, moving average, weighted moving average, exponential smoothing, double and triple exponential smoothing, and best fit.

I'd run the different models, and all would give me different forecasts for demand.

I would sit there and think, *which one is correct* and *are any of them correct*?

With so many different outcomes and variabilities to the forecasts, could I trust any of the models as being correct?

My real job at Oracle was in business analytics and intelligence, performance management and data warehousing.

I still have the Oracle presentations today where we were talking to clients about the transformation from reactive to proactive to predictive decision making with our analytics and intelligence platforms 20 years ago.

The point I am making is that going back many years, there was an interaction between a machine and a human where the machine was suggesting to me what my decision should be.

A few years later, I was VP Services with Atrion International, a regulatory compliance technology and consulting company.

Our regulatory technology platform was named Intelligent Authoring® (IA®).

Intelligent Authoring® contained regulatory content covering more than 50 countries in 44 languages, 300,000+ chemicals, 15,000 regulatory phrases, 5,000+ proprietary algorithms and 100+ regulatory forms.

Intelligent Authoring® was very advanced for the time with the 5,000+ proprietary algorithms.

When clients were first introduced to Intelligent Authoring®, they were blown away by the precision.

Many times, IA® produced regulatory content that the regulatory authors initially questioned.

Come to find out, IA® was smarter than most of the authors.

Authors are regulatory specialists who use IA® to produce material safety data sheets (MSDS).

Now, I will have to admit that IA® did make some mistakes, particularly when new regulations were being introduced.

Our Q&A team did a good job of testing IA®, but they did miss a few complicated combinations.

We built a collaborative relationship with our clients, who would help us flush out incorrect regulatory content.

Maybe a piece of regulatory content, or data, was incorrect. Or, maybe one of the algos needed tweaking.

It was the interaction of regulatory authors with IA® that enhanced the future of the intelligence of IA®.

We also utilized the power of the IA® platform for variety of predictive analytical modeling.

The point that I am trying to make is that these three examples are a historical reflection of what is happening today.

We are facing the same scenarios with AI. It is the interaction of an AI system with humans, and the development of the trust as to whether the AI system is providing the user the correct information to make an informed, bulletproof decisions.

The examples also show the use of advanced algorithms to support AI, ML and predictive analytics have been around for a while.

Your AI Experience

There is a tremendous and broader opportunity with AI, ML and RPA in our not-too-distant future.

Many organizations are already reaping the benefits of AI, ML and RPA.

We, as practitioners, have a new paradigm to use to understand how we will use AI, ML and RPA to more rapidly tackle business process optimization and transformation.

Instead of project-based, I can foresee continuous improvement on an ongoing basis, with regular self-correction of the processes.

We are seeing at a minimum, year-over-year double-digit growth in the investment in AI.

But before we get too far ahead of ourselves, let's look at using adoption in our own personal AI lives.

Siri and Alexa have made serious penetration into our everyday lives. However, AI technology is not perfected.

I will ask Siri: "Hi, Siri, can I have directions to blah, blah, blah."

Siri will respond: "Sorry but I cannot find any toad farms."

Deep breath and retry.

Me: "Hi Siri, can I have directions to blah, blah, blah."

Siri: "Getting directions to the Achileas Kousis goat farm in Athens, Greece. Is that the one you were looking for?"

Deeper breath and I am calling Siri names.

Does Siri mind personal insults?

No, I don't want to go to a goat farm! Did you not check my GPS coordinates? Greece, really!?!

My other favorites are the maps applications. A few years ago, a colleague and I were going to SAP headquarters in Newtown Square, PA. I had been there a few times but could not remember the exact directions from the Philadelphia airport.

I can't remember whether it was Apple or Google Maps I used for directions that day. After a short drive on the Interstate, we got off of the highway and entered the local streets. A few minutes later, I mentioned to my colleague, "This route does not look familiar."

He replied, "Don't worry. This is probably a faster way."

About a half-hour later, the maps app said, "You have arrived at your location. Climb up the hill."

What?

We were on some deserted country road with a big hill to our right.

The maps application wanted us to climb up the hill to get to SAP headquarters.

Trust me; this is a true story.

We all are experiencing our initial interactions with AI.

Do we have 100% trust in the recommendations?

No.

In another interaction with a maps app, you can look at the suggested route and wonder, *why in the world would I take that route? It makes no sense to me.*

As AI and ML increase their penetration into the business world, AI users are already experiencing the same challenges around incorrect information and trusting the system.

Have you ever:

Gotten frustrated with Alexa or a maps app to explain the rationale behind the recommendations?

Asked Siri or a maps app why it picked that particular route, but you didn't get an answer?

Have you ever:

Gotten frustrated with Alexa or a maps app to explain the rationale behind the recommendations?

Asked Siri or a maps app why it picked that particular route, but you didn't get an answer?

In a number of cases, a maps app has routed me through what I would consider dangerous locations.

As AI expands into areas with major impacts on us and our work lives, it will become increasingly vital that AI can explain why it has reached a particular decision.

The Siri example of getting your request wrong is that it just screwed it up. But what happens when you have to make a critical AI decision worth millions of dollars effecting people's jobs and lives? You won't be able to just screw it up.

I am a manufacturing specialist, so I will highlight some of the challenges I see with AI, ML and RPA in a manufacturing context.

The Foundation – AI and RPA Strategy

What is the company's AI and RPA strategy, and how do you plan to prioritize the AI and RPA projects?

Companies need to start by developing an AI and RPA strategy for the organization.

With so many areas of opportunity, companies need a solid strategy and roadmap as to where they will make their initial investments in AI and RPA.

Will the initial AI and RPA projects be in accounting, accounts payable or customer service?

What about product development, supply chain, manufacturing or maintenance?

There are so many choices ... and so few staff members and money.

Will the company go after an AI or RPA project with huge financial ROI but with significant risk and a potentially challenging implementation?

Or in the crawl, walk, run scenario matrix, will the company select a crawl approach with a project of high potential for success, and ease of implementation, but a not so great financial gain?

All of these strategy questions need to be flushed out with a clearly defined prioritization matrix.

And it's not just about financial return.

User acceptance and trust within the initial company's AI and RPA projects will set the impression standard for the organization when it comes to AI and RPA.

AI and RPA Impact on the Organization

I will start off with a brief story concerning an ERP implementation at a manufacturing company.

We were visiting one of the manufacturing plants on an educational tour and updating them on the timeline and impact the ERP implementation was going to have on the plant.

The rumor mill had already started by the time we got to the plant.

We had what I would consider a good meeting with the plant leadership team.

As we were discussing the change management workstream, the plant manager interjected a few thoughts. "You know, we have an aging workforce, and most of the people on the shop floor have very little education. They are extremely hard workers who produce great products for us with excellent quality. One of the machine operators stopped me the other day. He wanted to talk about the new fan-dangled computer system.

"He said, 'I have worked in this plant for more than 30 years. I take pride in making a great product. This company has been very good to me. But I hope you don't plan to try to turn me into no computer scientist!'".

Many of the plant personnel did not have Smartphones. At best they had the old flip phone. The consequence is that few if any, had experiences with the likes of Siri/Alexa and map apps.

As I have mentioned, ERP could stand for Early Retirement Program as well as Enterprise Resource Planning in many US manufacturing companies.

If ERP is an acronym for Early Retirement Program, is AI an acronym for Autonomous Intervention?

Meaning, will the introduction of AI in manufacturing plants mean another group is headed for the doors?

And how will companies find the new workforce of the future in manufacturing.

What will be the Pareto Principle effect on manufacturing organizations?

20% of the leading manufacturing companies will account for 80% of the early-stage AI and RPA deployments. The top 20% will suck up any available manufacturing/AI and RPA talent from the marketplace.

Meaning 80% of manufacturing companies may not be able to staff their manufacturing/AI and RPA needs.

This is already happening.

From an organizational culture standpoint, there will be new positions and personnel added to the organization to support AI and RPA.

Will your corporate culture support the addition of these new positions and people? Or will your culture look to these new positions as elite people of the 1%?

I have been involved with many corporate programs where a select group of individuals has been selected for a new cutting-edge business opportunity or project.

High profile transformation projects work best when the A-Players from the organization are tapped to be a part of the project team. AI and RPA will be considered a transformation project.

Will there be any backlash and jealously targeted at those individuals who get the AI and RPA assignment?

And how will outsiders be treated who join the organization for the AI and RPA transformation?

I've been on projects where the company has little to no experience with consultants. When we walk in the door, it's like a group of aliens has arrived. We are not looked at kindly.

Human resource leaders have a significant challenge ahead of them concerning their workforces of the future.

It is projected that as AI and RPA becomes mainstream and a greater part of the corporate fiber, 20–40% of the existing jobs will go away.

At the same time, the jobs in the future will require a reassessment of workforce design, with a new set of talent and skills in the workforce of the future.

Human resource leaders will not only be required to design these new workforces, but they will also be expected to develop talent pools and recruitment practices that align with the market place.

Human resource leaders will also have to rethink how they approach training.

Most companies conduct the initial training when a new employee comes on board or when a new technology is implemented.

This approach to single learning will have to evolve to continuous learning. And I am not talking about taking tests to make sure you can pass a test.

I am talking about new approaches to learning utilizing technologies such as virtual reality (VR) and augmented reality (AR). The workforce of the future will require these new approaches to continuous learning.

Sitting at a screen, reviewing slides and taking a test will not cut it with the workforce of the future!

Finally, what will be the incentives that your company offers to acquire the best available talent?

These are all questions that will need to be addressed to ascertain how the culture of the organization will handle the new positions and personnel.

AI and RPA Impact on Business Processes

There is great opportunity in AI and RPA for process improvements as it can monitor and adjust to many more variables, analyze data faster, and the AI and RPA logic should provide more objective and consistent recommendations.

The challenge I see with AI and RPA and business process optimization and transformation is that AI and RPA will lack a starting point.

I have not been on a business process optimization and transformation project where the existing processes are documented.

I am not saying every company lacks process documentation. What I am saying is that on my projects, there has been no current state process documentation.

Documenting the current state process is usually one of the first things we tackle on an optimization or transformation project.

If AI and RPA are going to optimize or transform a process, it needs a starting point.

Whether the optimization or transformation project is a business process or a new information technology implementation (ERP), current state processes don't exist.

When I optimize a process now, what is one of the biggest opportunities for optimization or transformation: hidden factories.

It usually takes a few iterations of the process maps to flush out all of the hidden factories.

But what I have learned is the without the current state processes, I have missed out on the hidden factories as well as other opportunities for optimization and transformation.

At some point in the not too distant future, AI and RPA will create the processes from inception.

Which brings me to another interesting obstacle that AI and RPA will face, how to integrate institutional and tribal knowledge.

Institutional and tribal knowledge is where most of the information resides. It is not documented but in the minds of individuals.

The question is, how will AI and RPA capture the institutional and tribal knowledge from all those individuals?

If you think today's digital transformations cause concerns about people losing their job, AI will be expediential.

Which brings up another interesting thought: What if the AI and RPA system is populated with incorrect or inaccurate information?

Let's give the AI and RPA system some bogus information and send it off on a wild goose chase!

I can see a bunch of people planning out bogus information to trick the AI and RPA system and then looking for the bad decisions and recommendations.

See, we told you the system sucks, and it can't be trusted.

Seems like we are getting back to the trust issue again.

There is no doubt in my mind; AI and RPA will have significant positive impacts on manufacturing.

Adoption and adaption issues will have to be addressed with openness and transparency.

AI and RPA Impact on Information Technology and Data

Manufacturing companies are some of the most behind of any industry with their technology infrastructure and ability to manage all the disparate data scattered around the organization.

Applying the Pareto Principle here, 20% of manufacturing companies are in a position where their technology architecture and data can take advantage of AI and RPA.

This means that 80% of manufacturing companies lack the technology architecture and mastery of data to take advantage of AI and RPA.

A friend of mine works for a US-based manufacturing company that builds systems and parts for some of the world's most advanced avionic technologies.

Yet his division is still on Lotus Notes.

I thought I would never hear that name again, never mind know someone whose company still uses Lotus Notes!

Lotus Notes databases, yikes!

Lotus Notes is a technology and data nightmare!

AI and RPA needs a robust technology platform and access to clean and available data.

AI and RPA systems live and die based on the quality of data.

In the 1984 commercial from Wendy's, Clara Peller, the 81-year-old actress, asked a question of Wendy's competitor's: "Where's the beef?"

This is one of the great classic commercials of all time that has transcended decades.

The AI and RPA system will continually ask: Where's the beef (data)!

If you don't have "the beef," the AI and RPA system will become another casualty for Shelfware.

AI and RPA impact on Performance Management

We spent an entire chapter discussing performance management and the need for accurate operational data.

When measuring the success of an AI and RPA initiative, you will be comparing the results against your existing KPIs and metrics that monitor the organization's performance.

Without an accurate "baseline" of existing performance, it will be difficult to measure the effectiveness of the AI and RPA initiative.

Some huge productivity gains are being unveiled around the success of AI and RPA initiatives. In some early examples, a 10X improvement in KPI performance was noted.

The recent advances in predictive analytics are uncovering data and information visibility that was previously hidden from view.

These are some of the game-changing results that are now being understood that validate the investments companies are making in AI, ML, RPA and PA.

Before your organization takes on an AI, RPA and PA project, you better have clean data and your performance management system better be in good shape.

AI and RPA Impact on Policies

The Organization for Economic Co-operation and Development (OECD) is an intergovernmental economic organization with 36-member countries that was founded in 1961 to stimulate economic progress and world trade.

The Committee on Digital Economy Policy of the Organization for Economic Cooperation and Development (OECD) plans to build on a proposed set of recommendations produced by a group of leading international experts to develop the first intergovernmental policy guidelines for AI by March 2019, with a goal of presenting a draft recommendation to the next annual OECD Ministerial Council meeting in May 2019.

With the rapid acceleration of AI taking place around the globe, there now appears to be an urgency to establish a set of intergovernmental AI policies.

This leads to the question, "What are the policies that are governing AI projects today?"

In the policies chapter, we discussed the need to understand the policies of your IT systems because the policies guide the behavior and decisions made by the systems.

I would suggest that policies concerning AI projects need to be clearly defined and understood.

I have learned that a significant challenge with current AI projects is the lack of visibility into how the AI decisions were made. Understanding the policies governing the AI system would greatly help with the visibility and trust issue.

Let's go back to our map apps example.

What are the policies that guide the route(s) that these map apps will suggest?

Are they only based on the calculated time to go from point A to Point B?

If not, what are the other policies producing for recommendations?

If you get three route recommendations, and all require the same amount of time, what are the other policies the map app is using to suggest Route 1?

I just made a map apps request from my home to International Plaza in Tampa, FL. Both routes would take 38 minutes, yet map apps made a suggestion as to its preferred route.

Why?

Now magnify this with a complex AI implementation which would be governed by a vast array of policies.

Know that the policies are important, whether in your regular IT systems or AI projects.

AI and RPA Impact
of Organization
Change Management

In change management, 20% are for the project, 20% are against the project, and 60% are in the middle and are undecided.

We'll most likely see the same with AI and RPA.

Based on our history with technology, the potential for job losses related to AI and RPA will be the #1 concern of employees.

AI and RPA will accelerate information flow and the spend to make decisions. This will make a certain group of the population uncomfortable. In particular, because of the lack of transparency in the decisions, AI and RPA presents.

AI and RPA are being touted for improving worker job satisfaction.

In some early examples, this has proven to be true.

As AI and RPA become more mainstream, what will be the long-term effect on worker job satisfaction?

As occurs with any change in process, the initial impressions will resonate with employees.

Bad initial experiences will be a big hill to overcome.

Companies need to make sure the initial AI and RPA experiences are positive. User testing with a select group of early adopters to flush out the learning pains will be critical.

Any large change initiative starts and ends with leadership from executives.

Executive leadership must empower managers to create a culture ready to handle AI and RPA.

New AI and RPA employees will be coming into companies, many in leadership positions in entirely new jobs that did not exist before the adoption of AI And RPA.

Executives will need to be able to explain to the organization the importance and need for these new employees to move the company forward for the benefits of all employees.

In the end, the success of large change initiatives comes down to the human element. The ability of humans to adapt to the changes, embrace the changes, and flourish with the changes in their new work environment will be paramount to the success of AI and RPA projects.

Summary

AI, ML, RPA and predictive/prescriptive analytics all offer tremendous opportunities toward the advancement of manufacturing as we know it, Industry X.0. As I write this book, Industry 4.0 is the current version.

History shows us that the introduction of any new or advancement in technology comes with its growing pains.

As I mentioned in the introduction, we see quantum leaps in technology every 5 to 10 years. Over the past two decades, we have experienced the adoption of eBusiness, Mobility, The Cloud, In Memory Computing and now Artificial Intelligence, Machine Learning, Robotic Process Automation and Prescriptive Analytics.

All of these advancements required companies to develop a strategy before proceeding with the implementations.

Some companies developed good strategies and quickly benefited from the advancements. While others did not develop good strategies and were and are, in many cases, still laggards.

AI, ML, RPA and predictive/prescriptive analytics all require a comprehensive strategy around the basics, organization, business processes, information technology, master and operational data, performance management and policies and organizational change management.

All of these leaps in technology have been massive transformational projects for companies to adopt. Let's not forget the challenges we have faced and the lessons we have learned over the past many decades when preparing for and implementing these amazing technologies.

CHAPTER 10

SUMMARY

I hope you have enjoyed this book and gleaned some valuable knowledge on how to execute business process optimization and transformation projects.

As you can see from the examples, organizations have a number of opportunities for business process optimization and transformation.

If you are early in your career or mid-career, this is a practical guide to the art and science of business process optimization and transformation.

What I have outlined in this book is what has worked for me across a variety of projects in a variety of industries at a variety of times during my career.

I did not start with this structure by any means; it has evolved over decades of work.

My goal is to accelerate your learning curve and equip you with the approach and tools to make you successful.

We are now at an enlightened inflection point in our society with the advent of a new level of power and maturity in AI, ML, RPA and PA.

The opportunities look to be limitless in our work in business process optimization and transformation.

Will the implementation be as easy as many claim? Only time will tell.

I see us facing many of the same challenges with any implementation of new information technology and also some new challenges that this earth-shaking technology will present us.

It always comes down to the interaction of humans with machines and how well humans learn to trust and respect the machine.

Until you have personally experienced an optimization or transformation project, it is hard for me to put the emotional IQ of what it takes in writing.

I have done my best to outline what has worked for me and to explain some of the pitfalls I have experienced over the years.

There are many twists and turns that a project can take, so not every project goes as planned.

What you expect to be the root cause of a problem may, in fact, only be a symptom of a bigger problem.

You have to have the inquisitive mind and analytical skills to get past the symptom and get to the root cause (s).

Sometimes what you find will be painful. Painful to the organization and painful to people.

Unfortunately, to correct processes and implement systems, everything will not be rose-colored glasses.

It can and will be an emotional roller coaster.

You have to prepare yourself, your project teams(s), executives and the organization of what is to come.

It is only through teamwork and respect for others that these projects get completed and deliver the results everyone is expecting.

Are these projects going to rub some people the wrong way?

Positively.

But you need to use your listening skills and understand where people are coming from on the project.

People are afraid to lose their jobs or have their jobs changed dramatically.

And in many, cases this will happen.

As I mentioned, these projects are emotional roller coasters with varying levels of stress and despair.

Plan well, be organized, communicate clearly and educate early and train often.

Most importantly, work hard to maintain respect.

Have fun solving your mysteries!

I love to solve mysteries!

REFERENCES

1. "Psychiatrist." Wikipedia. May 03, 2019. Accessed July 17, 2019. https://en.wikipedia.org/wiki/Psychiatrist.

2. Definitions adapted from Merriam-Webster Dictionary and Wikipedia.com.

3. "Scope Creep." Wikipedia. June 06, 2019. Accessed July 17, 2019. https://en.wikipedia.org/wiki/Scope_creep.

4. "Forming, Storming, Norming, and Performing: Understanding the Stages of Team Formation." From MindTools.com. Accessed July 17, 2019. https://www.mindtools.com/pages/article/newLDR_86.htm. Also, *Tuckman, Bruce W (1965). "Developmental sequence in small groups." Psychological Bulletin. 63 (6): 384–399.*

5. "Traditional to Scrum Team – Forming, Storming Norming and Performing." *Medium.* January 08, 2019. Accessed July 17, 2019. https://medium.com/@warren-2lynch/traditional-to-scrum-team-forming-storming-norming-and-performing-3fd5fd1f5ea9.

6. "PMBOK® Guide and Standards." PMBOK Guide and Standards | Project Management Institute. Accessed July 17, 2019. https://www.pmi.org/pmbok-guide-standards.

7. Kantor, Bob. "The RACI Matrix: Your Blueprint for Project Success." *CIO.* January 30, 2018. Accessed July 16, 2019. https://www.cio.com/

article/2395825/project-management-how-to-design-
a-successful-raci-project-plan.html.

8. Hayes, Adam. "Earnings Before Interest, Taxes, Depreciation and
    Amortization – EBITDA Definition." Investopedia. June 27, 2019.
    Accessed July 17, 2019. https://www.investopedia.com/terms/e/
    ebitda.asp.

9. "5 Whys: Getting to the Root of a Problem Quickly."
    Problem-Solving Skills from MindTools.com. Accessed
    July 17, 2019. https://www.mindtools.com/pages/article/
    newTMC_5W.htm.

10. Grief.com. Accessed July 17, 2019. https://grief.com/
    the-five-stages-of-grief/. Dr. Elisabeth Kübler-Ross, The
    Kübler-Ross Model, Elisabeth Kübler-Ross (July 8, 1926 – August
    24, 2004) was a Swiss-American psychiatrist, a pioneer in
    near-death studies and the author of the groundbreaking book
    On Death and Dying (1969), where she first discussed her theory
    of the five stages of grief, also known as the "Kübler-Ross model."

11. Ferris State University. *Grief Is a Normal Life Process.* Personal
    Counseling Center.

12. "About the Organizational Culture Assessment Instrument
    (OCAI)." OCAI Online Assess Organizational Culture Quickly,
    Easily and Reliably. Accessed July 17, 2019.
    https://www.ocai-online.com/

13. "Competing Values Framework Culture Model." OCAI Online
    Assess Organizational Culture Quickly, Easily and Reliably.
    Accessed July 17, 2019. https://www.ocai-online.com/blog/2017/
    Competing-Values-Framework-Culture-Model.

14. "4 Distinct Types of Corporate Culture-Which Is
    Yours?" L&D Daily Advisor. January 11, 2019. Accessed
    July 17, 2019. https://lddailyadvisor.blr.com/2018/0
    4/4-distinct-types-corporate-culture/.

15. Ibid.

16. Ibid.

17. Ibid.

18. https://en.wikiquote.org/wiki/Thomas_H._Davenport

19. The Stage Gate process is a registered trademark of Dr Robert Cooper.

20. Definitions adapted from Merriam-Webster Dictionary and Wikipedia.com.

21. "Pareto analysis." Wikipedia. https://en.wikipedia.org/wiki/Pareto_analysis

22. "5 Whys." Wikipedia. https://en.wikipedia.org/wiki/5_Whys

23. "Institutional Memory." Wikipedia. https://en.wikipedia.org/wiki/Institutional_memory

24. "Tribal Knowledge." Wikipedia. https://en.wikipedia.org/wiki/Tribal_knowledge

25. "Warehouse Management System." Wikipedia. https://en.wikipedia.org/wiki/Warehouse_management_system

26. "Vilfredo Pareto." https://en.wikipedia.org/wiki/Vilfredo_Pareto

27. https://www.gartner.com/en

28. "Serverless Computing." Wikipedia. https://en.wikipedia.org/wiki/Serverless_computing

29. "Performance Management." Wikipedia. https://en.wikipedia.org/wiki/Performance_management

30. Armstrong and Baron, (1998), Performance Management in Action, CIPD Publishing, ISBN 978-1-843981-01-5.

31. Robert S Kaplan and David P Norton, The Balanced Scorecard: Translating Strategy into Action, 1996.

32. Ibid.

33. "Performance Metric." Wikipedia. https://en.wikipedia.org/wiki/Performance_metric

34. "Illusion." Merriam-Webster Dictionary. https://www.merriam-webster.com/dictionary/illusion

35. https://www.gartner.com/it-glossary/advanced-analytics/

36. https://www.gartner.com/it-glossary/descriptive-analytics

37. https://www.gartner.com/it-glossary/predictive-analytics-2

38. https://www.gartner.com/it-glossary/prescriptive-analytics/

39. SAP, https://www.sap.com

40. Microsoft, https://www.microsoft.com

41. Tableau, https://www.tableau.com

42. Informatica, https://www.informatica.com

43. Alteryx, https://www.alteryx.com

44. "Policy." Wikipedia. https://en.wikipedia.org/wiki/Policy

Additional Resources
and Mentions

- 3E Company, https://www.verisk3e.com
- APICS (Supply Chain Operations Reference Model SCOR), https://www.apics.org
- Atrion International, https://sphera.com
- Global North LLC, http://globenorth.com
- Oracle Corporation, https://www.oracle.com
- Organization for Economic Co-operation and Development (OECD), https://www.oecd.org

ACKNOWLEDGMENTS

Authoring and publishing *I Solve Mysteries* have been an amazing journey.

From the day when the Lord put the thought of a book into my mind, to working with Silver Tree Publishing on becoming a published author, to having *I Solve Mysteries* listed on Amazon, I have really enjoyed the entire process of becoming an author.

I am thankful to so many people for their support during this journey.

To my wife and daughter, who loved and supported me through all the nights I have spent on the road and away from home, and who loved, supported and encouraged me while I was writing this book.

To my mother, Helen, for raising me with unconditional love.

To my dear friend, Al Pinney, for all of your love, friendship and guidance.

The team at Silver Tree Publishing is amazing and has been amazing throughout the entire publishing process. Many, many thanks to Kate Colbert, Penny Tate, Courtney Hudson, Hilary Jastram and Stephanie Feger. Thank You, Thank You, Thank You!

Special thanks to my editorial board — Jake Bishop, Peter Dragon, Jay McMahon, Tom Braatz, Tom McGrew and Nicole Lewis — who kept me on the straight and narrow and who provided valuable insights and ideas to make *I Solve Mysteries* the best book it could be.

My greatest appreciation to my book endorsers, George Kelley, Professor Michael Meeropol, Ray Leathers, Greg Williams and Chris Geissler for providing your outstanding and insightful endorsements.

Special thanks to Professor Meeropol, who taught me how to think with an inquisitive mind those many years ago as my economics professor at Western New England College.

To Bob Reed and Rob Biesenbach for guiding me to Silver Tree Publishing.

Thanks to Jason Ludwig for the great professional photographs.

Thanks to so many people I have worked with along the way in my career who have given me the opportunities to solve mysteries and who I have collaborated with in solving mysteries: Tom Braatz, Quave Burton, Mark Clark, Steve Crosnoe, James Davila, Rich Demarco, Don Dovgin, Scott Harter, Mike Hernandez, Keith Lavin, Patrick Lavoie, Wouter Monfils, Mike Notarangeli, Suman Purumandla, and Ram Shenoy.

Many, many thanks to the clients I have had the privilege to work with over my career. Each one of you helped me grow as a person and professional. Without you, there would be no *I Solve Mysteries*.

GO BEYOND
THE BOOK

Hire Dave Dragon and Dragon Management Consulting for:

Advisory Services

... that assist clients with understanding a practical approach to the rapidly emerging business and technology trends they are facing today.

Implementation

... rooted in discipline and collaboration, the true essence for a successful implementation of game changing business and technology solutions.

Education & Training

... that aligns the organization, business processes and digital technology focused on acceptance, competence and success.

The Dragon Difference

Businesses today are under tremendous pressure not only to deliver strong bottom-line results but to also implement advanced transformational process and digital technology solutions.

Dragon Management Consulting provides Advisory, Implementation, and Education & Training Services aligned with robust digital technology solutions.

- Artificial Intelligence/Robotic Process Automation
- Analytics & Insights
- Integrated Business Planning (IBP) / Sales & Operations Planning (S&OP)
- Operations
- Performance Management
- Supply Chain

Get the conversation started at 630.248.3375 or dave.dragon@dragonmcllc.com.

KEEP IN TOUCH

Dave Dragon

President, Dragon Management Consulting

📞 630.248.3375

✉️ dave.dragon@dragonmcllc.com

🌐 dragonmcllc.com

in LinkedIn.com/in/davedragon26
LinkedIn.com/company/dragon-management-consulting/

f Facebook.com/
Dragon-Management-Consulting-1925091941079085/

ABOUT THE AUTHOR

Dave Dragon grew up in Holyoke, MA, a rough and tumble industrial city along the banks of the Connecticut River in Western Massachusetts, and ultimately became a man whose questions get to the heart of the matter and whose interests lie in solving business mysteries and making leaders and organizations truly successful.

After obtaining his bachelor's degree in accounting from Western New England University, Dave began his business career at US Envelope, a division of Westvaco (now WestRock) in a finance management training program.

Dave's life and career path changed radically when he was transferred from rural Western Massachusetts to La La Land — Los Angeles, CA. It was at the US Envelope manufacturing plant in East Los Angeles, as Plant Cost Accountant, where Dave solved his first mystery providing the detailed analytics and insights used to turn around the operational and financial performance of the plant in less than six months.

Dave spent 17 years with Castrol, now part of BP, on a general management career track with increasing responsibilities in accounting, supply chain, sales and outsourcing. It was at Castrol where Dave solved the next mystery in *I Solve Mysteries* when he created an early version of Sales & Operations Planning (S&OP) while in his supply chain positions. During this time, he enhanced his consulting and change management skills with leading Fortune 100 manufacturers, implementing strategic operational excellence programs.

After obtaining an MBA in Strategic Management from DePaul University in Chicago, IL, Dave joined Oracle as a consultant in strategic enterprise management, business intelligence and data warehousing. Dave has always maintained he received an "honorary" master's in information technology while at Oracle during the go-go internet days. During his tenure at Oracle, Dave designed an early version of the technology solutions that today drive Integrated Business Planning or IBP.

Over the next many years, Dave held management and leadership position at a number of global technology and consulting companies, including Atrion International, Infosys and Hitachi Consulting, where he crafted his advanced skills in solving mysteries.

Dave currently leads his own consulting business, Dragon Management Consulting, which provides advisory, implementation, and education & training services in AI/RPA, Analytics & Insights, Integrated Business Planning (IBP)/Sales & Operations Planning (S&OP), Operations, Performance Management and Supply Chain aligned with robust digital technology solutions.

Dave resides in the Tampa, FL, area with his wife of 30 years, their beautiful daughter and handsome Wire Fox Terrier. Dave's interests outside of Solving Mysteries include rooting for his favorite Boston sports teams, golfing, traveling, food and wine (he's an accomplished chef), and exploring the beautiful coastline and waters of Florida.

In 2019, he published his first business book, *I Solve Mysteries: The Art and Science of Business Process Optimization and Transformation*, a foundational book for analysts and business practitioners across many industries.